AMERICAN LABOR

*FROM CONSPIRACY
TO
COLLECTIVE BARGAINING*

ADVISORY EDITORS

Leon Stein   *Philip Taft*

LABOR ARGUMENT IN THE AMERICAN PROTECTIVE TARIFF DISCUSSION

George Benjamin Mangold

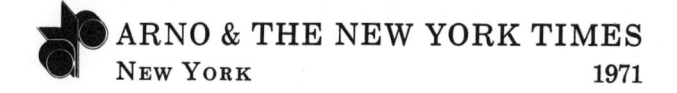

ARNO & THE NEW YORK TIMES
NEW YORK   1971

Reprint Edition 1971 by Arno Press Inc.

Reprinted from a copy in
The State Historical Society of Wisconsin Library
LC# 73-156433
ISBN 0-405-02931-4

American Labor: From Conspiracy to Collective Bargaining—Series II
ISBN for complete set: 0-405-02910-1
See last pages of this volume for titles.

Manufactured in the United States of America

ROOOO# BULLETIN OF THE UNIVERSITY OF WISCONSIN

NO. 246

ECONOMICS AND POLITICAL SCIENCE SERIES, VOL. 5, NO. 2, PP. 179-294.

THE LABOR ARGUMENT IN THE AMERICAN PROTECTIVE TARIFF DISCUSSION

BY

GEORGE BENJAMIN MANGOLD

Associate Director St. Louis School of Philanthropy

A THESIS SUBMITTED FOR THE DEGREE OF DOCTOR OF PHILOSOPHY
UNIVERSITY OF WISCONSIN

1906

Published bi-monthly by authority of law with the approval of the Regents of the University and entered as second-class matter at the post office at Madison, Wisconsin

MADISON, WISCONSIN
AUGUST, 1906

BULLETIN OF THE UNIVERSITY OF WISCONSIN

COMMITTEE OF PUBLICATION

WALTER M. SMITH, *Chairman*
WILLARD G. BLEYER, *Secretary*
FREDERICK W. MACKENZIE, *Editor*

THOMAS S. ADAMS, *Economics and Political Science Series*
WILLIAM H. LIGHTY, *University Extension Series*
WILLIAM S. MARSHALL, *Science Series*
DANIEL W. MEAD, *Engineering Series*
EDWARD T. OWEN, *Philology and Literature Series*
FREDERICK J. TURNER, *History Series*

CONTENTS

	PAGE
CHAPTER I.—INTRODUCTORY	9
1. Growth of Commerce	10
2. Character of Export Trade	11
3. Manufactures	12
a. Attitude toward their Increase	14
(1) Position of Calhoun	14
(2) Hamilton's Report on Manufactures	15
(a) His argument in Reference to Labor	16
b. Development of Manufacturing Industry	18
CHAPTER II.—LABOR PROBLEMS CONCERNED IN THE TARIFF QUESTION	20
1. Statement of Problems	20
2. Women and Children	21
a. Importance in Industry	22
b. Industries affected	22
c. Relation of their Employment to Tariff Act of 1816	24
3. Scarcity of Hands and Unemployment	25
a. Causes of Scarcity	25
b. The Mechanic	26
c. Machinery	27
d. Early Conditions of Unemployment	28
e. Crisis of 1819–20	29
(1) Intensity of Crisis	30
(2) Unemployment occasioned	32
(3) Effect on Tariff Policy	32
4. High Wages of Labor	35
a. Cause	35
b. Comparison between American and Foreign Wages	36
c. Wages of Women and Children	38
d. Rise of American Wages	40
5. Immigration	42
CHAPTER III. –THE DEVELOPMENT OF THE LABOR ARGUMENT TO 1824	46
1. Nature of Opposition to Manufacturing	47
a. Political Objection	47
b. Moral Effect	49
c. Other Grounds of Opposition	50
d. High Wages—A Hindrance	51

CONTENTS

2. Argument for Protection................................. 54
    a. Unemployment emphasized........................ 55
    b. High Wages minimized............................ 55
    c. Immobility of Labor............................. 56
3. Summary... 57

CHAPTER IV.—THE DEVELOPMENT OF THE LABOR ARGUMENT AFTER 1824... 59
1. Intrusion of Land Question............................ 59
    a. Argument of Rush................................ 60
    b. Attitude of Benton.............................. 61
2. Immigration of Artisans.............................. 62
3. Women in Factories................................... 63
4. Tariff and Wages..................................... 64
    a. Gallatin on Wages............................... 64
    b. Attitude of Southern Men........................ 65
    c. Free Trade Convention of 1831.................... 67
5. Evolution of Protectionist View-point................. 68
    a. Decline of Opposition to High Wages.............. 68
    b. Security of Employment demanded................. 69
    c. Protection to Labor............................. 71

CHAPTER V.—FACTORS AFFECTING THE LABOR ARGUMENT. 73
1. Former Indifference to Condition of Laborer.......... 73
2. Beginning of the Labor Movement...................... 74
3. Demand for Higher Wages.............................. 75
4. Crisis of 1837....................................... 76
5. Growth of Idealism................................... 79
6. Immigration.. 80
7. Political Importance of Laborer...................... 80
8. Summary.. 83

CHAPTER VI.—THE RISE OF THE PAUPER LABOR ARGUMENT. 84
1. Increased Attention to Interests of Laborer.......... 85
2. Demand in 1832 for Protection against Foreign Labor.. 86
3. Nature of Arguments presented........................ 87
4. Convergence of various Movements makes Pauper Labor Argument important.................................. 89
5. Horace Greeley....................................... 91
6. Debate on Tariff of 1842............................. 92
    a. Argument of Protectionists...................... 94
7. Whig Platform in 1844................................ 95
8. Attitude of Advocates of Free Trade.................. 97
    a. South slow to recognize need of high wages...... 98
    b. Calhoun and Walker.............................. 98
    c. Wages and Land.................................. 101

[182]

CHAPTER VII.—CONCLUSION	103
1. Review of Development of Argument	104
2. Importance of Rise of Laboring Classes	104
3. Sectionalism	105
4. Development of Wage Theory	106
5. The Logic of the High Wage Argument	108
6. Protection and Wages	109

PREFACE

The purpose of this paper is to indicate the labor difficulties involved in the early development of our manufacturing industries and the plans suggested for their solution; to show how these difficulties affected the tariff problem; to analyze the character of the labor argument employed in favor of the tariff; to picture the social and political conditions giving rise to it; to show how a well-differentiated laboring class affected the nature of the argument advanced by both protectionists and free-traders, and to trace the development of the pauper labor argument for protection.

THE LABOR ARGUMENT IN THE AMERICAN PROTECTIVE TARIFF DISCUSSION

CHAPTER I

INTRODUCTORY

To understand the importance and intricacies of the labor argument as first employed, it is necessary to review briefly the character of early American industry. The adoption of the constitution of the United States was not only a self-conscious movement toward greater political security but was in part an effort to ameliorate the depressing economic and industrial conditions which prevailed throughout a large part of the country. Commercial unrest was, in fact, one of the chief causes contributing to the formation of the constitution. Under the new government greater industrial stability was hoped for. It is well known that the determined stand of Boston mechanics for the constitution, because they believed that under it they would receive a greater degree of protection against foreign goods, contributed vitally to the ratification of the constitution by the state of Massachusetts.

Agriculture was at that time the predominant American industry. It was the occupation of the great majority of Americans, and by far the most important source of wealth. In 1790 only 3.35 per cent. of the population lived in cities of 8,000 or more, thus showing the comparative unimportance of cities, and the great preponderance of agricultural industries. Even as late as 1820 more than 80 per cent. of our people were engaged in agriculture. Wealth was not concentrated in cities, and large numbers of the rich owed their wealth to the possession of vast landed estates. In fact, the men of wealth in our national legislature were quite uniformly members of the landed classes, and our early legislation cannot be understood apart from this important fact. Physiocratic ideas had exercised a profound influence upon American thought and the importance of agriculture was still largely over-estimated. Many men believing that our economic welfare would thus be best preserved, hoped we would remain an agricultural country. Others looked with trepidation upon the observable signs of a comparative increase of manufacturing interests. Jefferson himself, a large land holder, held, in the main, to the old notions, and his influence was potent in the councils of the nation.

Commerce, however, was not a negligible fraction of our industrial interests. Its importance was increasing very rapidly, and protection was early extended to it; for American vessels only were allowed to engage in our coasting trade. An impetus was thus given to the shipping interests and an additional effort was made to increase the tonnage engaged in foreign trade. This was conspicuously successful, as the following facts indicate: in 1808 the figures were 14,000 and 110,000, respectively, for the tonnage of British and American ships sailing between the two countries, against 72,000 for England and 21,000 for America, in 1789.[1] Continual warfare in Europe and the injury which it inflicted on the shipping interests of the various countries gave America an advantage of tremendous value, and in 1807 her ship tonnage had mounted to the magnificent sum of 1,089,876.

Napoleon's attempt to destroy British commerce and the political measures which it entailed, both here and abroad, for a time seriously crippled our thriving trade, while the war of 1812 was another serious and distinct blow. A gradual recovery from this depression was followed by a decline in 1821-22, but by 1823 the same level was attained which prevailed in 1811, the tonnage for the year amounting to 775,271.[2]

---

[1] Gibbins, H. de B., *Economic and Industrial Progress of the Century*, 55.
[2] *Annals of Congress*, 42: 2263.

Our commercial interests had plainly assumed considerable importance. In 1820 as many as 80,000 American seamen were employed in our carrying trade. Our merchants were the dominating influence in a number of our seaports, such as New York, Boston, and Charleston, which were not only centers of political activity, but controlled the politics of their respective states. This industry wielded a political power far in excess of its proportionate importance among the principal industries of the nation and the shaping of our economic policy was to a considerable extent contingent upon its attitude.

The character of our early export trade has an extensive bearing upon the outcome of our protective policy and indicates some of the causes for sectional differences on the subject. Cotton was one of the principal exported articles. The capital employed in its cultivation in the United States was about $80,000,000 in 1801, and was continually increasing.[3] About 100,000 persons were employed in growing it or depended upon it. There were about 900,000 slaves in the United States at that time and the cotton-gin had come into use, so that a rapid extension of cotton culture was practically assured. Tobacco and rice were southern products. Indian corn was raised both in the South and in the North, while meat and lumber were largely confined to the latter section. Our average yearly export of grain and flour during the period 1790–94 was 1,421,335 barrels; for the period 1821–23 it was only 1,177,949 barrels. The exports of raw cotton rose from a value of $5,000,000 in 1800 to $20,000,000 in 1823. In the year 1800 our total exports amounted to $47,473,000 or about $8.00 per capita. In 1820 they were $51,683,000 or virtually $5.00 per capita, while the figures for 1823 were $47,155,711 and $4.00 respectively.[4] There had been waves of increase and decline, commerce having suffered from the Embargo Act, the War of 1812, and the crisis of 1819–20, but the general tendency seemed unfavorable. During the year 1820 manufactures to the amount of $3,000,000 were exported, but the raw materials exported, exclusive of cot-

---
[3] Bishop, *History of Manufactures*, **2**: 88.
[4] *Ann. of Cong.*, **42**: 2125.

ton and wool, were less by $18,000,000 than their aggregate for 1800. It was claimed that this loss fell upon the northern and middle states, while the South alone was gaining. Undoubtedly there was reason in this complaint; besides this, many men in the North believed the South to have an advantage in its slave labor. The large foreign trade of the South, on the other hand, strengthened the commercial interests of both sections to such an extent that both desired its expansion. It was thus with increasing interest that the North observed the growth of manufacturing interests and the application of artificial means to achieve their further advancement.

Manufacturing, however, concerns us most, as it was in connection with this rapidly rising branch of industry that the tariff was largely discussed. It was here that the labor problem first became acute and demanded solution. We were far behind England in the value of our products; yet we manufactured flour, distilled spirits, linen goods, tanned leather, molasses, iron products, ships, etc. Hats were an important article of manufacture and the wool used was largely of domestic growth. The material for glass could be secured in large quantities, but considerable manual labor, numbers of skilled workmen and large capitals were required for the successful pursuit of the glass industry.[5] In all of these particulars the nation was but inadequately furnished. Flour and spirits were manufactured in the same regions that actually produced the supply of grain. There was as yet no system of internal improvements and few facilities for transportation, hence bulky matter was usually transformed into finished products before shipment to market. Even then a slight depression of trade or fall in prices necessitated untold hardships to farmers and to the so-called manufacturers. Such conditions eventuated in the Whisky Rebellion and other movements of discontent.

The erection of a cotton mill in Rhode Island in 1791 and the advent of Samuel Slater were portentous events in the history of American manufactures, and hence were important factors in the determination of our subsequent tariff policy. Woolen mills

[5] Bishop, *History of Manufactures*, 2: ch. 1.

were also erected and strenuous efforts to make them successful were made, but not until the War of 1812 and later was much accomplished by them. Difficulties of various kinds continually arose. Besides this the habits of our people conspired to cause their failure, for the greater portion of all woolen goods used north of the Ohio river were manufactured within the families themselves after the manner of the old domestic system. In fact, as late as 1828, when the tariff on wool and woolens was so largely agitated, this condition was still essentially unchanged. Long after machine production had begun to assume considerable importance in certain industries, the old domestic system by its persistent lingering delayed the advent of a manufacturing era. Despite these facts, considerable advance was being made, as will be subsequently shown.

Having concluded this preliminary statement, let us note the general attitude held toward the development of industry, and its early progress during the time when it was not affected to any appreciable degree by protective legislation. Most of our prominent statesmen, though not entirely free from sectional bias, still believed in a broad national policy. The landed interests, powerful in the nation's councils, naturally emphasized the importance of agriculture, but favored such policies as would conduce to greater general prosperity. This, it was believed, would be enhanced by a parallel development of manufactures along with that of agriculture and commerce. Agriculture would always remain the predominant industry of the nation, but progress along all lines was desired. Even before the adoption of the constitution, Tench Coxe extolled the advantages and resources of America; spoke of her varied sources of wealth, and of the need of systematizing our industry to attain the maximum of advantage; and argued that the three great industries would naturally arise under such conditions and should be properly correlated.[6] Physiocratic doctrines, however, were not yet dead, and Hamilton, in his report on manufactures, found it necessary to defend manufactures against the charge of inferior

---

[6] *Address to Friends of American Manufactures, in Univ. of Pa.*, Aug 9, 1787, 31.

productiveness, and to assert in their favor that they occasioned "a positive augmentation of the produce and revenue of society."

More and more, however, the development of the backward manufacturing industry was viewed with complacency and positive approval. It was argued that we should encourage the manufacture of products necessary for our national defence. If possible we should be independent of foreign nations in this respect. Washington advocated such a policy. Madison, while president, urged similar measures, although originally a free-trader at heart.[7] He advanced beyond this and deliberately recommended the encouragement of such manufacturing industries as the nation was fitted to carry on with success after they had been established and efficiently pursued.

This broader attitude toward the proper development of American industries found ample expression during the first important struggle over the tariff question in 1816. The lines of political cleavage had not yet definitely separated the North and South into two opposing sections. However, both nationalistic and sectional influences externalized themselves in this contest. Eminent statesmen, such as Calhoun, clung to the idea of national expansion and national greatness, and sectionalism was less prominent than it subsequently became. Hence we have in the following words of Calhoun a clear statement of the national view-point of the men of the earlier generations—a view-point which comprehended the growth of the entire nation along many lines rather than that of particular sections only.[8] "Neither Agriculture nor Manufacturing nor Commerce, taken separately, is the cause of wealth. It flows from the three combined and cannot exist without each.—Without Commerce industry would have no stimulus; without Manufactures it would be without the means of production; and without Agriculture neither of the others can subsist. When separated entirely and permanently they perish. War in this country produces, to a great extent, that effect and hence the great embarrassment that fol-

[7] *Messages and Papers of the Presidents,* 1: 567.
[8] Calhoun, *Works,* 2: 166.

lows in its train. It is admitted by the most strenuous advocates on the other side that no country ought to be dependent upon another for its means of defence;—But what is more necessary to the defence of a country than its currency and finance? Behold the effect of the late war upon them! When our manufactures are grown to a certain perfection, as they soon will be under the fostering care of the Government, we will no longer experience these evils. The farmer will find a ready market for his produce, and what is almost of equal consequence, a certain and cheap supply of all he wants. His prosperity will diffuse itself to every class in the community, and instead of that languor of industry and individual distress now incident to a state of war and suspended commerce, the wealth and vigor of the community will not be materially impaired."

Thus we get a glimpse of early industry in America. We find the three great industries existing side by side. All are flourishing, but the domestic manufacture of certain imported articles is earnestly desired. More than that, general national development is hoped for, and this desire causes national interest to attach itself to the subject of the tariff and its relations to the manufacturing industries of the nation.

The period immediately following the organization of the new government was not marked by any desire on the part of our national law-makers to interfere extensively with the natural trend of American industry or to give special and artificial encouragement to our manufacturing system, which was then in its infancy. The existence of millions of acres of wild, uncultivated, low-priced land had a tremendous effect in retarding the development of the factory system, and with the agricultural advantages which obtained, it was natural that free labor apart from the farms should be scarce.

The obstacles which manufacturing industries had to face are stated by Alexander Hamilton in his celebrated *Report on Manufactures*.[9] The most important one is "dearness of labor." This, he says, has relation principally to two circumstances:

    1. Scarcity of Hands.
    2. Greatness of Profit.

---
[9] *American State Papers. Finance,* 1: 123 ff.

"The disparity between some of the most manufacturing parts of Europe and a large proportion of the United States is not so great as is commonly imagined. It is less in regard to artificers and manufacturers than in regard to common laborers. Disparity is diminishing as greater use can be made of machinery. Wages furnish but one of a number of items in the cost of goods. We have an advantage in some of them. Foreign goods pay certain extraordinaries. These cannot be estimated at less than 15 or 20 per cent., and are more than a counterpoise for the real difference in the price of labor."

In regard to scarcity of hands, he argues that increased use could be made of women and children, and opportunity would be given in manufactures for the employment of persons ordinarily engaged in other occupations during their seasons or hours of leisure. In addition to this argument against the alleged difficulties confronting success in American manufacturing enterprise, he summed up the advantages which would accrue from such industry, maintaining that the produce and revenue of society would be greater than it would otherwise be, owing to the following circumstances:

1. Division of Labor.
2. Extension of the Use of Machinery.
3. Additional Employment for classes of the community not ordinarily engaged in the business.
4. Promotion of Emigration from Foreign Countries.
5. The Furnishing of Greater Scope for diversity of talents and dispositions which discriminate men from each other.
6. The Affording of a more ample and various field for enterprise.
7. The Erecting in some instances a new, and securing in all, a more certain and steady demand for the surplus produce of the soil.

A glance at Hamilton's argument at once discloses his keen appreciation of the need of a large labor force. The problem of establishing manufactures was mainly a question of how to secure a sufficient number of hands and to best utilize all of our available laboring population. The home market argument which later swayed the West and was for a time the chief reliance of protectionists is also mentioned. Nothing is said, however, and little is intimated about the need of protection to American capital. To be sure, Hamilton advocates protection but not the artificial construction of industry. Rather, he seeks a policy which will result in the employment of all laborers to the best advantage.

The development of manufactures was sought, then, by the first great advocate of the manufacturing system along natural and economic lines. It must be remembered, also, that conditions and ideals differed from those prevailing later. Women wove and spun and made goods in their own homes. Their transition to a common workshop where a number together performed the same work as was done in the homes, with the advantage of additional machinery, was not only not generally opposed but commended. The employment of children was regarded as neither uneconomic nor injurious. In short, agriculture and commerce failed to employ our labor force to the best advantage. Much valuable time was entirely wasted, and much labor power was completely lost. In part, the development of our manufacturing industries would add an important by-product to the wealth of the nation. This by-product was to be secured by simply applying all of our available energies to the production of manufactured goods. The objection, that Hamilton favored a restrictive system which was calculated to transfer labor power from the more to the less productive enterprises, is not valid. The labor supply is indeed an important factor with him, but he would not take labor from the fields nor from the ships and the ocean. Sufficient idle labor existed to justify the nation in encouraging manufactures, for if these odds and ends were employed, great economic advantage would certainly result. Hamilton saw that the comparatively few industries in which Americans engaged offered little opportunity for diversity of talent; he felt that a greater variety of interests could be obtained and that this would conduce to the increase of national wealth. Furthermore, he looked with favor upon the increase of immigration, as adding to the labor supply of the country and giving us new power for the extension of manufacturing enterprises. In short, the difficulties with which the country had to contend as far as convenient, sufficient, and qualified labor was concerned, formed the subject of Hamilton's argument. It was exactly these difficulties that he believed could be obviated, and the institution of a protective system seemed to him to be capable of accomplishing this object, without limiting the industries already established in any way, but by supplementing them with otherwise unemployable labor.

In spite of the fact that Hamilton's recommendations received insufficient support, and although low tariff rates only were imposed, and these with but slight reference to current American industries, still the progress of manufacturing continued, and the factory system began to develop. Some encouragement, it is true, was desired for its development by other leading statesmen, as before indicated, but on other grounds than those urged by Hamilton. Furthermore they did not advocate the system so strongly as he did.

Natural progress, the aid of European wars, the commercial blockades instituted by France and England, and other accidental circumstances, gave impetus to American manufactures and transferred capital from commerce to the former industry. By 1810 we had developed our manufactures to considerable proportions, as the excellent and exhaustive report of Tench Coxe amply demonstrates. In his analysis of the available returns, he estimated the extent of American manufactures, excluding articles which he classed as doubtful, in the following manner:[10]

Total Amount $173,762,676
Total for Penn. 33,691,111
Total for N. Y. 35,370,988
Total for Mass. 21,895,528
Total for Va. 15,203,473
Total for R. I. 4,196,074
Total for Conn. 7,771,928

The value of the doubtful articles amounted to $25,850,795 and included such items as: hemp, fish, salt-peter, sugar, etc. If this

---

[10] *American State Papers. Finance,* 3: 712, 713.

figure is added to that representing the value of bona fide manufactured goods, a total of more than $198,000,000 is reached. This, Coxe showed, compared very favorably with England which manufactured annually about $250,000,000 worth of goods. The report enumerates the principal special industries and values the output of each as follows:

Textiles (woven and spun) $41,549,000
Hides and Skins 17,935,000
Iron 14,364,000
Liquors 16,528,000

The facts indicate that remarkable progress along manufacturing lines had been made, there having been no government interference, although the extraneous circumstances above mentioned doubtless accelerated activity in these industries.

With manufacturing carried on to such an extent, naturally a large number of laborers had to be employed, and a laboring class was slowly differentiated from the other classes of society. The size of this class at that time is not definitely known, but the census of 1820 states the number engaged in manufacturing as 349,000 approximately, and a large amount of goods were made by persons who were not included in this enumeration. So the actual number of persons who sympathized with the efforts of labor was undoubtedly larger. Strikes and labor difficulties occurred, to some extent, as early as the first decade of the century, but during these generally prosperous years comparatively little disturbance was occasioned. It is at a later period, after the War of 1812 and the end of the Napoleonic wars, that new industrial conditions, causing hardship to America, gave form to the struggle of labor and added to the self-consciousness of the growing laboring class. It was under such conditions, when the old system was not yet forgotten and the new industrial régime hardly inaugurated, and when contradictory situations abounded everywhere, that the discussion of a protective tariff in 1816, and later, involved the labor question. At this time arose the series of arguments, which, on one side, finally culminated in the pauper labor argument; and, on the other, in the claim that wages stood upon an independent basis.

CHAPTER II

LABOR PROBLEMS CONCERNED IN THE TARIFF QUESTION

To understand the rationale of the early argument concerning the tariff and its relations to labor, it is necessary to be conversant with the following facts, for each has a decided and distinct bearing upon the question.

1. The existence of several industries (cotton, woolen, etc.) in which the employees were recruited largely from the ranks of women and children or from labor which would have been idle otherwise.

2. The comparative dearness of male manual labor; that is, high wages and a frequent scarcity of hands.

3. The immigration of skilled mechanics from abroad and the constant encouragement by Americans of this class of immigrants.

4. The rapid rise of machine industry.

5. Taste for certain classes of industry by particular individuals and their consequent dislike for other kinds of labor.

6. The accidental but important displacements and periods of enforced idleness caused by sudden disarrangements of the industrial system; e. g., the crisis of 1819–20, which almost without warning, thrust upon the country the difficult problem of general unemployment and in a concrete way demanded a solution of the difficulty.

7. Finally, sectional interests and a natural clash among different sections for industrial advantages; also alliances between sections to obtain certain desired ends.

The above named facts profoundly influenced the current thought of the people, and assisted in moulding their ideas in respect to proposed legislation. Each general fact regarding industry and the labor difficulties involved, called for treatment in concrete form and apart from general theoretical and abstract considerations. An examination of the foregoing statement of conditions will show their bearing upon the questions of the day and especially upon the labor difficulties to be solved by protection or to be aggravated by it.

Women and Children

The employment of women and children in industry was one of the most important factors which hastened the advent of our protective system. As already stated, the domestic system still prevailed largely in the textile industries and a large proportion of the goods of this character which were consumed by the American people, were manufactured by the women in their homes; so it did not appear to be a revolutionary proposal to utilize their labor in manufacturing establishments devoted to the production of the same class of goods as they had been making under the old system. Here was a large volume of potential labor capable of successful utilization. The meager educational facilities and opportunities for women favored such a step. The daughters of thousands of farmers and many women in the cities saw in these industries a new field for gaining a livelihood; or at least felt that part of the year could advantageously be spent in the service of a textile manufacturer. The effect of the introduction of factories of this kind upon the work of women is indicated, in part, by the following facts.

Gallatin, in 1810, gives a short account of both domestic and factory industry.[1] Speaking of household manufactures in New Hampshire, he says, "Every farmer's house is provided with one or more wheels according to the number of females. Every second house, at least, has a loom for weaving linen, cotton, and coarse woolen cloths which is almost wholly done by women. Manufactures, per family, vary from 100 to 600 yards per year, without an hour's loss of labor to the field. Much coarse flaxen

---

[1] *American State Papers. Finance*, **2**: 435.

cloth, worth 15 to 20 cents per yard and manufactured in families is sold to traders and sent to the Southern states." Besides enlarging upon the value and importance of the goods manufactured under the domestic system, and the fact that no labor was lost through these efforts, he prophesied, on the basis of the known facts for the year 1810, that in 1811 there would be 87 cotton mills containing 80,000 spindles in operation. These would employ 4,000 persons, of whom 3,500 would be women and children, and only 500 of the entire number would be men.[2]

It is undeniable that the development of manufactures was a goal to be sought for. We were importing a large amount of finished goods, the raw materials of which were to a large extent produced here or easily capable of production. Hence the practical question confronted American statesmen—how can labor power be secured to carry on these industries without sacrificing the productiveness of the industries already established? Gallatin was deeply concerned about the utility of the labor of women and children, and was unwilling to injure the profitable and growing industries of agriculture and commerce. Tench Coxe was even more radical. In discussing the cotton industry, he expressed the following sentiment.[3] "Our maximum of exportation of cotton in any one year is 64,000,000 pounds. This would produce 50,000,000 pounds of yarn and require the work of 58,000 persons. Of this not more than one-eighth ought to be adult males, the other seven-eighths might be women and children. This employment of less than a hundredth part of our white population would be no inconvenience to agriculture or to commerce. This yarn could be produced with ease by 100,000 women with the fly shuttle, during one-half of each working day in a year." His comments on the woolen industry are equally significant. "The manufactory of hats, consuming more wool with few hands than any other of the ancient modes, is carried to the extent of our consumption. . . . Female aid in manufactures, which prevents the diversion of men from agriculture, has greatly increased. Children are employed as well as the infirm and crippled . . . The asylums of

---
[2] *Ibid.*, 427.
[3] *Ibid.*, 669.

the poor and unfortunate and the pentientiaries of indiscretion and immorality are improved and aided by the employment and profit of manufactures. In the section of the Union occupied in part by colored laborers, decent and comfortable hospitals have been established upon some of the planter's estates, in which children, convalescents, aged persons, and married females . . . have been employed with humanity and advantage in manufacturing cloths and stuffs for apparel and furniture."

In England more than 1,000,000 people of both sexes and all ages were employed, in 1816, in the cotton and wollen manufactures. Four-sevenths of the cotton employees were women and children. Such facts were cited as examples of our own possibilities. Idleness was held in disfavor and unnecessary leisure regarded as a waste of our economic power. The Philadelphia Society for the Promotion of Domestic Industry well illustrates this point of view.[4] It called particular attention to the desirability of employing persons who would otherwise be idle, on account of temper, habit, or other causes. It claimed, furthermore, that women and children were rendered more useful by being employed in manufacturing establishments. It argued, in addition, that factories would give employment to classes of the community not ordinarily engaged in the business, but who are willing to devote their leisure time, resulting from the intermission of their ordinary pursuits, to collateral labors as a resource for multiplying their acquisitions or their enjoyments.

Popular feeling and economic conditions thus combined to give added support to the cotton industry. After 1815, however, the industry began to be depressed, owing largely to increased competition from abroad; and manufacturers appealed to the nation for assistance. A congressional investigation was instituted and the following report was the result:[5] The capital invested in cotton manufactures in the United States was estimated at $40,000,000. The number of laborers reached 100,000,

---
[4] *Address*, 62.
[5] *Rep. of Com. on Commerce and Manufactures*, in *American State Papers. Finance*, 3: 32 ff.

of whom 10,000 were males seventeen years and upward, 66,000 were females, and 24,000, boys. The total wages paid annually amounted to $15,000,000 and 81,000,000 yards of cotton were manufactured. This report indicates the importance of woman and child labor at that time, which affected not only the general labor supply but sometimes resulted in making families dependent upon their children for support.[6] The maintenance of a livelihood having become easier for many parents, they naturally were interested in the continued growth of the industry.

The conspicuous feature of the tariff act of 1816 is the protection it afforded to cotton goods. The duty was fixed at 25 per cent. and was to remain so for a period of three years. The system of minimum valuation was applied and no cotton cloth was to be rated at less than $.25 per yard. The purpose of the act was largely to protect the capital invested in this industry but subsequently other industries were protected. It is significant, however, that the industry employing the greatest proportion of women and children was the first one receiving important protection, nor should it be forgotten that the employment of women and children and its advantages received considerable attention and was a part of the labor phase of the tariff discussion, which became so important later.[7]

In the woolen and other textile industries the same kind of labor was employed and it was only after 1820 that Irish immigration began to displace the English and American girls in our factories.[8] There was little or no controversy over their employment, and their labor was regarded as an addition to the wealth of the nation. The higher duty on cotton goods was undoubtedly more easily secured owing to the predominance of female labor in that industry. The extensive employment of child labor also made possible a rapid increase of industry along certain other lines. Not only had the textile industries been invaded but the manufacture of tobacco and paper was accelerated in this way, the wages paid to children being compara-

---

[6] Batchelder, Samuel, *Cotton Manufacture*, 74.
[7] *American State Papers. Finance*, 3: 18, 23.
[8] Depew, *A Hundred Years of American Commerce*, 29.

tively low.[9] The labor of women and children was a decided factor in establishing a number of our industries.

SCARCITY OF HANDS AND UNEMPLOYMENT

These two factors played a large part in the tariff discussions of the early protection period. Hamilton, as we have seen, pointed out the disadvantage due to scarcity of hands but tried to minimize its effect. In fact the attitude of protectionists was quite uniformly that of Hamilton, while free-traders emphasized and perhaps magnified these features of American wage conditions. No wonder then that an appeal was made in favor of manufactures and the protective system on the ground that the sons of farmers were unemployed during the winter, and that they would gladly utilize their labor power in factories during this period. Scarcity of hands was a real problem to the friends of American industry. There was a definite class of seamen. The mechanical trades were also important and the labor difficulties of the first decade of the century pertained largely to these classes. A well differentiated manufacturing or factory class, however, did not yet exist. The rapid growth of the western states continually aggravated the difficulty, while the slower growth of the eastern and landless states indicates the course of migration. Between 1790 and 1820 the increase in the population of Massachusetts averaged about 11 per cent. per decade; that for Rhode Island, Connecticut, Delaware, and Maryland was considerably less; while states with large areas of unoccupied land—such as New York, Pennsylvania, Maine, and Ohio—showed a tremendous increase. Agricultural pursuits were too attractive and too remunerative to permit the formation of a very large male manufacturing class. The dangers and trials of the wilderness deterred many, it is true, from migrating westward and this fact helped to swell our manufacturing population, but the hardy and ambitious young men preferred to become land holders. Therefore our people were largely engaged in agriculture and little skilled labor existed,

---
[9] *Accounts of Manufacturing Establishments.* Washington, 1823.

but in a few industries exceptional progress had been made; for example, in the manufacturing of hats. In this industry we had excelled for a long time and to such an extent that by 1814 we were actually exporting hats in considerable quantities.

In certain other industries, such as have already been named, considerable proficiency had been acquired but, in the main, there was a dearth of skilled labor and this deficiency had to be supplied, in part, by the independent skilled mechanic who was both laborer and capitalist, or by the importation of goods from abroad.

The mechanical trades were represented by a small variety of artisans; chiefly carpenters, blacksmiths, shoemakers, and such others as ministered to local wants.[10] Not only were they numerically important, but were also influential factors in the life of the community. Auburn, New York, with 2,047 inhabitants in 1818, had 74 mechanics' shops and 211 dwellings.[11] Ithaca gave similar proportions. Mechanics were numerous everywhere but often mechanical art was an avocation only, while agriculture was the chief occupation. For example, one-third of the male inhabitants of Hall county, Georgia, were artificers or workmen of some kind, but most of them relied upon agriculture.

The mechanic differed from the ordinary laborer. He was usually an independent producer and possessed capital of his own. He was furthermore regarded as more or less skilled. Mechanics and laborers, however, belonged to the same general class, and it is only later that a sharp differentiation took place, the interests of the mechanic being the first to receive attention. In the tariff debate of 1820 this class is mentioned as forming one of the parties entitled to consideration in the laying of tariff duties, and from that time on the interest of the mechanic in the tariff question is apparently considerable. The mechanical trades supplied the need for labor to a certain extent only and the general difficulty still remained. Mechanics were loath to change from their old independence to the new conditions of factory life, and in but comparatively few cases was it possible to rise

---

[10] Stanwood, *American Tariff Controversies*, 1: 17.
[11] *Darby Tour*, 219.

to factory ownership and to the position of employer. These facts caused those interested in the development of manufactures to turn to such measures as were available, so as to provide a labor supply adequate to meet the new needs and demands. The problem of skilled labor was not easy to solve. The industrial revolution in England had produced a series of striking changes, of which the effects of new machinery were most important. Machinery was a prime factor in solving the problem of manufactures in that country.[12] It was estimated that in 1808 the diminution of manual labor in the cotton industry by means of machinery was as 200 to 1.[13] In America, indeed, machines for printing cotton and woolen cloth were in operation. 10,000 yards could be printed in a day by one man and two boys. The general scarcity of labor and comparatively high wages gave a decided impetus to invention. Our patent laws, though defective, had received some revision and great progress was made under them. During the single year of 1812 there were 237 patents granted in the textile industries alone.[14] By 1814 hundreds of carding machines had been introduced in New York; wool picking machines were used; the fly shuttle was being multiplied and many European improvements were employed. The tariff controversy of 1816 brought out the declaration that "a great proportion of the woolen manufacturing is done by the assistance of labor-saving machinery, which is almost exclusively superintended by women and children and the infirm who would otherwise be wholly destitute of employment."[15] Two ways of solving the problem of manufactures are suggested here, while the inference that general hands were scarce can be clearly drawn. It is undeniable, however, that England excelled us by far in the machinery which she was enabled to utilize and that she had advanced in the industrial arts to a much greater degree than manufacturers in America. A large part of England's ability to produce goods cheaply lay in her possession of good labor-saving machinery—an advantage

---

[12] Philadelphia *Advertiser*, Nov. 6, 1819.
[13] *American State Papers. Finance*, 2: 669.
[14] Levasseur, *American Workman*, 25.
[15] *American State Papers. Finance*, 3: 164.

which we could not overcome for many years. In 1824 Henry Clay estimated that machinery did the work of 221,000,000 men in England, but in America that of 10,000,000 men only.[16] This was a tremendous handicap, but the physical and economic conditions of America soon started us on the way toward improvements and inventions of all kinds, and, coupled with the well-known American ingenuity, finally gave us a preeminent position. At that time, however, the question of machinery was a serious problem and materially impaired the comparative efficiency of our laboring population.

With such conditions existing, it seems contradictory to assert that the problem of unemployment was an important factor in protective legislation. Unemployment and scarcity of labor cannot exist side by side, yet both factors contributed to the discussions of the tariff. In this connection two things must be kept in mind; first, the fact that the friction of travel and the inconveniences incident to migration were so great that labor might be abundant in one section and quite scarce in another; and, second, that crises, or the sudden disarrangements in industry, with their accompanying depression might turn thousands of men out of employment and deprive them of a means of gaining their livelihood.

Unemployment has the immediate effect of drawing attention to the concrete situation with the result that the theoretical considerations are largely abandoned and a temporary policy adopted. The positive and concrete side of the protective controversy has had an almost invariable advantage. The fact of the existence of a general depression has had an important influence upon the enactment of three protective laws. The crisis of 1819–20 measurably affected the tariff legislation of 1824; the depression commencing in 1837 and lasting several years helped to determine the Act of 1842, and the hard times of 1893–96 culminated in the Dingley tariff of 1897.

Before the inception of our protective tariff system, unemployment was but a minor phase of American industry. Foreign competition, however, proved disastrous to many of our manu-

---

[16] *American Sentinel,* April 14, 1824.

factures, and frequently other causes cooperated to injure them. England tried to prevent the exportation of machinery to America in order to retain her market here. False standards of custom had arisen and frequently a foreign article was preferred to the equally serviceable American product. Some of the states had given protection to certain industries before the adoption of the Constitution, and the removal of interstate barriers injured such industries. Again, foreign skill was largely superior to that acquired by Americans.

These causes tended to produce considerable unemployment or depression from time to time. Accordingly appeals were made to the government for aid. Manufacturers, mechanics, tradesmen, and "others" frequently asked Congress for relief, for a change in the tariff schedule, and for such duties as would again bring prosperity.[17] Petitions were received from all the important cities during the first year of the new government and in subsequent years requests for help were continually made.[18] While Congress gave but little encouragement, it is significant that aid was hoped for from that quarter.

The increasing unemployment following the year 1816 and culminating in the great crisis of 1819-20 gave a powerful impulse to our tariff policy and popularized protection in many parts of the union. The return to peaceful pursuits of thousands of European soldiers at the close of the Napoleonic wars, England's attempt to break down our manufactures, the inflation of American currency, and other causes contributed to the serious maladjustment in our industrial system. The year 1818 had been apparently prosperous. Building was carried on at a rapid rate. Evidences of a boom were in the air. Mechanics, carpenters, and masons were in great demand. New York City could not supply its needs. Even journeymen could not be procured at the rate of $2.00 per day and hundreds more could have found employment. The farmers were receiving good prices and enjoyed a large degree of prosperity. Flour rose to exorbitant figures and other products followed.

The sudden panic coupled with the increase of imports par-

---

[17] Bishop, *op. cit.*, **2:** 15.
[18] *American State Papers. Finance,* **1, 2.**

alyzed American manufactures, and a rapid fall of prices followed. Although cotton had been protected, many cotton factories perished, those equipped with the best machinery surviving. Rents and the value of real estate depreciated. Farmers sold lands at one-half or one-third of their value. Vast numbers of handicraft workmen entered into competition with the farmer, thus increasing the product although there was practically no market. It was estimated that real estate in New York fell 18 per cent. between 1815 and 1821, while the expenditures for the relief of paupers nearly doubled.[19] Pennsylvania and Rhode Island also suffered severely. The depression in cotton had occurred in 1815–16 and a similar distress was felt in Pittsburg during the latter year.[20] Two-thirds of its population was engaged in manufacturing, thus accentuating the keenness of the depression. Most of the flour of western Pennsylvania found a market here and much bacon was brought from the West. The distress among the laborers lessened the ability of the farmers to dispose of their surplus products, a fact which gave an added impetus to the home market argument for protection. Conditions grew worse, however, and by 1819 had become almost intolerable. The major portion of the laborers in this locality were out of employment, and the situation in Philadelphia was no better. An investigation in the latter city revealed the fact that the number of laborers employed had decreased from 9,425 in 1814–16 to 2,137 in 1819.[21] A fall in the weekly wages from $58,340 to $12,822 is also recorded, indicating the degree of distress which must have prevailed. The cotton, woolen, and iron industries had been almost entirely wrecked, while other industries suffered greatly. Poverty in Pennsylvania was wide spread and the actions for debt taken in the courts of that state within the single year 1819 amounted to the almost incredible number of 14,537.[22] Imprisonments for debt in the city and county of Philadelphia alone rose to the number of 1,808.

---

[19] *Ann. of Cong.*, **42:** 2074.
[20] McMaster, J. B., *History of the People of the United States*, **4:** 344.
[21] *Address before Philadelphia Society for Promotion of Domestic Industry*, 11.
[22] Carey, M., *Olive Branch*, 133.

The total amount of unemployment throughout the country can only be estimated. In a single year, says Denslow, 70,000 operatives were discharged and driven into idleness or agriculture.[23] Thousands, it is true, turned to farming and did not remain idle. Bishop estimated that from 40,000 to 60,000 persons were thrown out of employment during these years and that 160,000 to 240,000 were deprived of support. During 1819-20, however, the crisis was most acute and at least 30,000 persons were divested of employment, of whom many were said to have been reduced to poverty or compelled to break stones on turn-pike roads at $.25 to $.37½ per day.[24]

Such an extraordinary crisis necessarily exerted a profound influence over the opinions of the people. The manufacturing population was sufficiently large to impress its importance upon the popular mind. By 1820 both Massachusetts and Rhode Island employed one-half as many persons in manufactures as in agriculture. Pennsylvania stood third with 42 per cent. and other states had made considerable advance.[25] How these facts affected the growth of protection is shown by the events of the immediately ensuing years.

About 1817 the first important society for the promotion of American industry was established at Philadelphia. Composed in part of manufacturers, it had, however, for its moving spirit Matthew Carey, who first awakened public attention to the need of a system of internal improvements in Pennsylvania, who favored a system of free, universal education, and who labored long and energetically for the poor. During the years 1818-22 he wrote a large number of essays appealing to the people of America to adopt the protective system. His discussions covered the entire range of available arguments and they throw light on prevailing conditions and the general sentiment of the people. Carey pointed to the desperate condition of the American people and included in his enumeration the statements that from one-third to one-half of our merchants were ruined, that thousands of our workmen were idle and that the city officials

---

[23] *Economic Philosophy*, 381.
[24] *American State Papers. Finance*, 3: 493.
[25] *Census of 1820.*

of Philadelphia, after canvassing the situation, concluded that the unemployed in that city alone numbered 11,000.[26] He emphasized the low wages which many workmen received and computed that probably 150,000 manufacturers or descendents of manufacturers (laborers) were tilling the soil in western states and in the interior of New York and Pennsylvania who, under a proper system, would still be engaged in manufacturing. Besides calling attention to the starving condition of many recent immigrants, he lamented the fact that many of our citizens had migrated to Cuba to recover from their disasters. Carey drew a striking contract between the prosperous conditions which prevailed at the close of the war and the lamentable state of industry and the distress of the years of the panic and depression. The emphasis which he placed upon the fact of unemployment was peculiarly apropos to the existing state of affairs, and his proposed remedy was therefore fitted to receive considerable attention. To revive prosperity he desired an extended application of the principle of protection. He believed that the protective tariff would again enable us to utilize our idle capital, to build factories, and that it would give employment to the thousands who were idle or were laboring for a bare pittance.

His appeal for protection had a wide-spread influence, laborers especially being struck with the argument concerning unemployment and the method of relief. After 1820 his writings began to be studied more carefully and the younger men also gave considerable attention to the lives of Hamilton and Franklin,—a fact which strengthened their views on the tariff. The severity of the panic and the concomitant growth of protection literature left a lasting impression upon the people of Pennsylvania. Since 1820 they have been unflinchingly in favor of a protective tariff. In fact, as a single cause giving impulse to protection sentiment, the crisis of 1819–20 was one of far-reaching consequences.

Carey's efforts were seconded by men everywhere. Citizens of Philadelphia adopted resolutions deploring the prostrate

---

[26] Carey, M., *Essays on Political Economy*, 198, 233, 441, etc.

state of manufactures, the unemployment of the workingmen, and their reduction to mendicity. One resolution stated that no candidate for the state legislature or for the Congress of the United States would receive support from them unless such candidate was known to be friendly to the protection of domestic industry.[27]

State legislatures took up the discussion and inquired into the cause of the great depression and hard times. The legislature of New York declared in 1820 that the influx of foreign goods had destroyed the credit of many country merchants and was breaking up our manufacturing establishments; that thousands of our laborers were thrown out of employment, and that many had become a public charge. In this way the cause of protection continued to gather volume. Even Tammany Hall was affected. To a large extent it drew its support from the class of people who were thrown out of employment. In deference to the sentiment of these adherents, it issued an address in 1818 favoring a moderate protective tariff, but it was later forced by the shipping interests and merchants to return to the advocacy of free-trade.

Other signs of the times are noticeable in the fact that 30,000 persons throughout the middle and eastern states memorialized Congress for relief.[28] In Congress stress was laid upon the propriety of enacting legislation for the benefit of large classes of people who were suffering from want. The tariff bill of 1820 failed, however, but this fact must be attributed not to the triumph of the opposite principle but to the successful opposition of merchants and planters who believed that their prosperity depended upon free-trade. The argument against the constitutionality of protective legislation had been mentioned before but as yet had little weight. It gathered its impulse in the South, but only after it became apparent to that section that protection was an injurious policy in respect to her industries, and an advantage to the remainder of the Union. The labor side of the tariff controversy in Congress at that time is well represented by Baldwin of Pennsylvania, who voicing the well

---
[27] *Niles' Register,* **17:** Sept. 4, 1819.
[28] Carey, *op. cit.,* 387.

crystallized sentiment of that state said, "Hundreds, thousands of our citizens are out of employment. They would add infinitely to the national wealth, to our independence, and save its resources at home if their labor was employed in converting our raw materials into fabrics for our own use."[29]

The mechanic whose interests were not regarded as identified with those of the manufacturer received the following fulsome praise from another speaker. "The cardinal interests to be supported by the government appear to be agriculture, manufacturing, commerce, navigation, and that of the mechanic. . . . . It is not confined to great cities, of which it forms the bone and gristle, but has its stand of influence and respectability in every village and agricultural section of the nation."[30]

Echoes of the influence of panic and depression were heard in 1824 when Clay, who as the representative of the West relied chiefly upon the home market argument for protection, stated, "The truth is, no class of society suffers more in the present stagnation of industry than the laboring class. That is the necessary effect of the depression of agriculture, the principal business of the community."[31]

Baldwin and Clay were spokesmen for two sections. The evil of unemployment was felt more heavily in the East, that of agricultural depression in the West. Hence the former emphasized the labor argument while the latter subordinated it to the demand for prosperity in agriculture. That the subject of enforced idleness was still widely exploited is clear, however, from the remarks of Webster, who at that time was still a freetrader.[32] "We do not need work for hands," said he, "but hands for work. I do not find those idle hands of which the chairman of the committee speaks. Capital solicits labor; not labor, capital. The mere capacity to engage in agriculture gives our young men independence."

The attention paid to the subject of unemployment by prominent partisans in the tariff controversy clearly indicates that

---

[29] *Abridgement of Debates,* 6: 607.
[30] *Plain Sense on National Industry,* 47–48. New York, 1820.
[31] Speech in Congress, March 30–31, 1824.
[32] *Ann. of Cong.,* 42: 2063.

consideration for the laborer was beginning to be necessary. The crisis of 1819–20 had developed a more serious side of the growing labor problem and helped materially to pave the way for the more complete development and evolution of the labor argument for protection.

HIGH WAGES OF LABOR

Turning to another side of the labor situation, we find that protectionists had considerable difficulty in reconciling their positions, and that the variety of economic conditions made consistent argument difficult, at least until the various points contributing to the argument could be carefully selected, properly correlated, and then reared into a permanent structure. A brief review here of the general facts regarding wages will suffice to point out the line of the development and the subsequent change in the character of the argument.

The reputed dearness of labor in the early decades of the nineteenth century was a comparative, not an absolute, fact. Compared with the wages paid to English and continental laborers, the American wages were far superior. On the other hand, the wages paid in the United States have increased almost steadily since 1800, progress having been interrupted only by crises and depressions.

These high wages, the extent of which Hamilton tried to minimize, and which manufacturers bewailed, were closely dependent upon the amount of free land accessible to the American laborer. The amount of land was practically unlimited. It could be secured on easy terms, was fertile and insured its possessor a life of independence and a considerable competence. The American people were accustomed to pioneer and wilderness conditions, hence migration to the West was not a dreaded alternative for the larger number of laboring men of the East. The earnings of the western lands roughly determined the wages of labor. Consequently the price of labor was comparatively dear. Our manufacturers were at a disadvantage. England was the chief competitor in our own markets, and had the advantage of low wages and good machinery. Furthermore she exerted herself to retain this market, by prohibiting the exportation of machinery, by stringent emigration laws, and in other ways. High wages was a difficulty not easily counteracted by other mitigating forces.

Wage conditions in England made it possible for that country to place goods upon the market very cheaply. Gibbins[33] says that between 1800 and 1845 wages for both manufacturing artisans and agricultural laborers were very low, that for some thirty years the wages of weavers were often under fourteen shillings per week and sometimes even less than five shillings, and that from 1830 to 1845 they ranged from thirteen to seventeen shillings for men and from seven to nine for women. Prices for wheat were very high, and little butter, cheese, bacon, tea, or sugar was consumed by the working men. The rapid increase in her population, bad poor laws, and other causes kept wages very low, much lower than the ordinary American manual laborer was willing to accept.

There were several classes of labor, however, whose rates of wages must be distinguished from each other. These were common and agricultural labor, that of women and children in factories, that of unskilled men in mines and factories, and that of the skilled mechanic. Even a brief survey of wage conditions with the scattered data at our command, indicates the appalling lack of appreciation of higher standards of life. The high wages of the second and third decades of the century seem contemptibly low today, yet as late as 1842 Calhoun spoke of high wages as a drawback to the development of American manufactures.

The wages of agricultural labor stood comparatively high in 1818, as did that of other labor, and allowance must be made in comparing this rate with the wages subsequently paid. According to an estimate made in 1832[34] the average rate paid in the principal New England states and New York in 1818 was $10.00 per month. In Pennsylvania, Maryland, the extreme South, Southwest, and the far West of that day the rate was higher, being $11.00 in the first state and rising as high at $15.00 in Missouri. In Virginia and North Carolina $6.00 was

---

[33] Gibbins, *Economic and Industrial Progress of the Century*, 347.
[34] *Congressional Debates*, 8: 217.

the rule, and for Ohio the paltry sum of $9.00 is recorded! By 1826 wages had fallen nearly 10 per cent., every locality contributing to the decline. The rate continued stationary for some years, 1830 showing but little change. The comparatively high wages of agricultural labor of the sparsely settled states, Missouri excepted, had, owing to increased immigration, been slightly reduced, but Pennsylvania and New Hampshire showed gains, while New York paid but $8.00 per month. Wages in Massachusetts seem to have risen from $8.00 per month in 1815 to about $11.00 in the following two decades. These were high wages compared with those paid during the latter part of the eighteenth century. The depression of 1819–20 affected the wages of farm labor, many persons having been thrown out of employment. Clay in 1824 estimated the wage of able bodied men at from $5.00 to $8.00 per month. The daily wage was somewhat higher, an average of $.75 being regarded as a proper figure. It varied considerably within the same state, however, and also with the seasons. Harvest wages of $1.12 and board were reported in 1819. The rest of the year the rates were much lower, often but $.50 a day, and during the following winter no other consideration than that of board and lodging was hoped for in many parts of the United States. The general stagnation had affected agricultural as well as other labor. As long as transportation facilities were inadequate the farmer of the interior could not hope for high prices for his produce nor pay wages which compared with those prevailing in other lines of work. The subsequent opening of canals made higher wages possible in the territory tributary to the new waterways, and additional facilities of travel tended to raise the wage of the farm hand. On the whole, however, the reputed high wages of labor were high only when compared with the price of foreign labor. In 1825[35] the monthly rate in England was but $6.50 and that in France varied from $4.00 to $6.00, while the price of wheat in both countries far exceeded the American figures. Labor on the turnpikes received wages similar to those in agriculture, $.50 to $.75 per day was a cus-

---

[35] *Report on the Statistics of Labor*, (Mass.), 1885, 180.

tomary price about 1828. Henry Carey estimated $.78 to $.80 as the usual wages of the laboring man between 1820 and 1830, and that eleven days' labor was sufficient to obtain a quarter of wheat, although the labor of sixteen days was required in England to secure a like quantity. Such conditions of advantage were the cause of the complaint in regard to high wages, and in the absence of better ideals, this view-point is easily understood.

The labor employed in factories received various rates of remuneration. The transition to the factory system carried with it a large amount of woman and child labor. The wages paid were high enough to tempt only this class of labor into industry. In 1812, boys of sixteen were frequently employed at no more than $.42 per week. The congressional committee which in 1816 investigated the cotton industry estimated the average annual wage of the employees at $150. The majority of these were women and children, so that probably a higher rate for children than the one mentioned above obtained at this time. In 1832[36] the operatives in this industry were paid an annual wage of approximately $154. The wages of men were estimated at $5.00 per week, those of women at $2.00 and of boys at $1.75. While before the advent of the factory system the ordinary price of women's labor was $3.00 and less per month, and board, now it was more than doubled. From $1.75 to $2.00 per week were the prevailing rates for women during the thirties and by 1840 even boys received as much as $2.00 and board,—a figure considerably higher than that formerly paid.

The investigation of industrial conditions in Philadelphia in 1819[37] revealed rates of wages which in 1816 varied from $3.12½ to $9.00 per week and averaged $6.20. The lowest wage was paid in the woolen industry, while in the textiles, in general, the lower rates prevailed. Male adult labor, however, received as much as $7.50 per week in certain cotton factories, although the average here was considerably less, being perhaps about $5.00 during the second and third decades of the century. Yet free-traders pointed assiduously to the reputed dearness of

---

[36] Carey, H. C., *Essay on Rate of Wages*, 69.
[37] *Address before Phila. Society for the Promotion of Domestic Industries*, 11.

labor, claiming that wages were 100 per cent. higher here than in England, thus making competition in manufactures impossible. The iron industry in Pennsylvania employed a large number of men and with its increasing importance became implicated in the tariff discussion. About 1820[38] the wages paid to the iron operatives varied but little from $200 per annum. Similar statistics for certain New York establishments indicate a yearly wage of about $250, but other states yielded less favorable results. By 1832 wages had risen and an average of $300 per year was reported. Figures based upon the census returns of 1840,[39] however, indicate that the average wages paid in that year had reached a per capita total of $365. Wages in the coal industry were a matter of some importance in view of the controversy over the duties on coal. In the spring of 1836[40] miners received $7.00 per week and owing to extraordinary competition for men the rate subsequently rose to $2.50 and $3.00 per day. Foreign workmen were promised at least $1.00 per day for every working day in the year if they would come to America and enter the mines. Thus it appears that the price of labor in the coal mines corresponded closely to the wages paid in the iron industry.

The wages of mechanics, many of whom took strong ground for protection during the first period of active protectionism, underwent considerable variation during the same time. Henry Carey[41] estimated the wages of carpenters and bricklayers in the years 1783–90 at from $.62½ to $.75 per day, but in 1834 the wages of the former were $1.12½ to $1.25, and of the latter $1.37 to $1.50 per day, although the average price of wheat was less in the later period than before. Pittsburg shoemakers in 1815 received from $9 to $12 per week and paid $2 to $3 for board. In 1818 mechanics—carpenters, blacksmiths, cabinet makers—and tailors about Philadelphia received from $9.00 to $11.25 per week. The persons employed in the more necessary

---

[38] *Digest of Accounts of Manufacturing Establishments.* 1823.
[39] Convention of Home Industry. 1842.
[40] *24th Cong., 2d Sess.; Sen. Docs.,* **1**, No. 59.
[41] Carey, H. C., *Essay on Rate of Wages,* 26.

trades were well paid, but others fared less favorably, thus occasioning important migration for want of sufficient employment. The extensive building before the crisis of 1837 operated to enhance the wages of carpenters and allied trades, many of whom were securing $2.00 per day. The crisis,[42] however, seriously affected the earning power of large numbers of our laborers and mechanics, thus paving the way for a renewed demand for higher wages. With carpenters and masons enjoying wages 50 per cent. higher than those paid in England, the American mechanic had a decided economic advantage but furnished the selfseeking manufacturer an adequate basis for complaint.

In spite of predictions to the contrary the price of labor was higher in 1840 than at the beginning of the century. The movement of prices was, on the whole, favorable and thus contributed to an increased real wage for the laborer. The increasing facilities for agriculture coupled with better machinery accelerated the steady rise of wages. Farm labor was affected by the growth of manufacturing industry, which apparently tended to increase the wages of the former. The comfortable wages paid in industrial sections point to that result. The free lands of America, on the other hand, gave us one incalculable advantage over Europe, and made it impracticable to pursue any industry which could not afford high wages unless unnatural conditions interfered or protective legislation was adopted. Henry Carey, writing in 1835, recognizes the comparative dearness of labor in America. He further points out its greater productivity and maintains that our female factory employees received higher wages than the average amount paid to men, women and children in the English cotton mills. Yet in comparing the various classes of laborers with those in England he finds a smaller advantage in our favor than do the ardent free-traders of the same period.[43] The crisis of 1837, however, threatened the high wage of the American laborer, and the miserable conditions prevalent in England depressed the wages of her operatives to shamefully low levels. The contrast between the two countries was accentuated, and not only our

---

[42] *Log Cabin,* Sept. 26, 1840.
[43] Carey, H. C., *op. cit.,* 81.

superiority emphasized, but the necessity of our retaining a high standard for our working men was duly insisted upon. In addition to wage rates already given, paper manufacturers now paid $6.00 to $9.00 per week, and the average wage in cordage establishments in Massachusetts was $1.06 per day. Our glass workers received much higher wages than the prevailing rates abroad. English testimony shows that, in some cases, the wages of man, wife, and two children, all engaged in the cotton industry, were about equivalent to the sum obtained by a well paid female operative in America where high wages were receiving greater appreciation. The fact that wages were higher in the North than in the South vitally affected the tariff question. While $20.00 to $25.00 was paid per month by northern operators, $15.00 only was paid in the South for similar work. The free labor of the North was receiving good wages, while southern labor, suffering from an obsolete industrial system, was placed at a disadvantage. A comparison with the prices of foreign labor therefore became more complicated and explains in part the divergent views held upon this question.

To summarize, it is apparent that the wages of mechanics were highest; that the early dearness of labor had not abated, but was gradually increasing; that female employees and children were gaining ground; while agricultural labor, although practically stationary during the third decade, subsequently improved its condition. Relatively high wages was a fact, hence the tariff could not leave it out of consideration. These facts were responsible for certain definite results. First, only those industries could succeed in America whose productivity was very great, and in which, therefore, high wages could be paid. Our machinery must be good and our labor skillful, otherwise competition would be impossible. In both cases we experienced considerable difficulty. Second, cheaper labor was used wherever possible, thus introducing women and children into the factories, and encouragement was given to the immigration of labor from abroad, especially that possessing some degree of skill. Consequently the actual rate of wages paid was of less importance in tariff discussion than the relation between wages here and abroad.

IMMIGRATION

The defects in our industrial system were so great that skilled labor from abroad was heartily welcomed. As we have already stated, America had certain disadvantages, one of them being a dearth of hands skilled in certain industries which we desired to develop but which so far had not been vigorously prosecuted on that account. The immigration of skilled mechanics and artisans from abroad was earnestly sought to fill up this gap in American industry.

Tench Coxe in his summary of the manufacturing industry, pointed to the fact that no branch of manufactures received so large an accession of foreign workmen as the woolen industry, because the raw material and its manufacture were so universal in Europe. Progress in this industry was especially hoped for through further immigration. In 1816 woolen manufacturers, in petition to Congress, again suggested the advantage of development along these lines. After indicating the gain resulting from the employment of classes unfitted for agricultural pursuits, they called attention to the importance in this industry of valuable foreigners who at home had been solely engaged in manufacturing. The fact that England had attracted immigrants in former years and through them built up a number of her own industries was cited as an example of our possibilities. Artisans and skilled laborers were needed, and as late as 1827 Secretary Rush said that under a proper manufacturing system we might reasonably expect to see a new class of immigrants coming to the United States; that not only unemployed journeymen from foreign work-shops but master manufacturers with capital would come and that they would stimulate our industry and hasten our progress.[44] Matthew Carey,[45] writing at the time of great depression, feelingly expresses a similar view in the following words: ''Thousands and tens of thousands of artists, mechanics, and manufacturers, with talents beyond price and many of them with handsome capitals, escaped from misery

---
[44] *Report on Finance, 1815–1828*, 404.
[45] Carey, M., *Olive Branch*, 238–9.

and oppression in Europe and fled to our shores as a land of promise where they expected to find room for the exercise of their industry and talents. They sought employment at their usual occupations. None was to be found. Numerous instances have occurred of cotton weavers and clothiers, etc., who have sawed and piled wood in our cities and some of them have broken stones on our turnpikes for little more than a bare subsistence. Many hundreds have returned home, heartbroken and lamenting their folly. . . . Many of those who have been unable to return, rendered desperate by distress and misery, have proved injurious to the country to which they might have produced the most eminent advantages." As spokesmen and friends of American industry, both Rush and Carey point plainly to one of our difficulties and disadvantages, and in so doing suggest the connection between the protective tariff and the encouragement of immigration.

Our early immigration was not extensive and England retarded it somewhat. Her laws allowed vessels from Great Britain and Ireland to carry to our shores only one passenger for every five tons burden, but it was permissible to carry a passenger for every two tons burden if the vessel were bound for other ports than our own. This law did no great amount of injury, for the immigration of the first quarter of the century was largely English and Irish, and the law was subsequently repealed. We welcomed these men and societies were organized to take care of newly arrived immigrants even before the close of the eighteenth century. It was for economic reasons mainly that we desired this addition to our population, and the first objections to immigration were based upon political grounds. But the problem of the establishment of manufacturing industries was to be partially solved by inducing foreigners to come among us, and the tariff was to be used as a means to that end.

As for the occasional labor which might be employed in manufacturing, a word may be profitably added. Industry was still in a state of instability. Many important features of the old domestic system were still retained. A large proportion of the labor was not continuously employed in the same industry and many were idle when they might have been advantageously employed. Such a waste seemed needless, and ardent friends of manufactures hoped to utilize this economic power. In 1816 the regular employees in the woolen industry were estimated at 50,000 and those occasionally employed at the same number. The ratio here given is quite significant and indicates another source of labor.[46] The small factories and the prevailing desire of the majority for pecuniary advancement accentuated this species of employment, and made possible the argument used by Hamilton and by later protectionists. Never a very strong argument, however, it soon lost its force as economic conditions changed and sharper differentiation among laboring and industrial classes took place. Still this argument of occasional labor cannot be entirely neglected, for the woolen industry, which later became the subject of considerable tariff legislation, depended partly upon this particular kind of labor.

In conclusion it is clear that a general scarcity of labor prevailed in the manufacturing industry. Agriculture and commerce had made extreme demands on the labor supply. The unfortunate depression after the War of 1812, however, so disarranged industry that an excessive amount of unemployment obtained for a number of years. The ideals of the times were such that the people instead of disapproving of woman and child labor, not only favored but encouraged it. Its importance in the cotton industry cannot be overlooked. The same is true of the irregular labor engaged in the woolen manufactories. The bearing of the need of skilled artisans and mechanics, of the demand for better machinery, and of the encouragement given to immigration, must also be considered in discussing this side of the tariff question.

Finally, the fact of high wages stands out pre-eminent. In spite of unemployment and crises and the temporary depression of wages caused by these conditions, a normal wage comparatively high continued to maintain itself. Actual wages tended to approximate to this standard which was far above that of European countries and hence gave our manufacturers considerable trouble.

---

[46] *Address before Philadelphia Society for the Promotion of Domestic Industry,* 86.

The facts and conditions above named, differing for different sections, added to the chaos of argument in respect to the protective tariff. With emphasis, however, placed upon the subject of wages, and with a more consistent correlation of the other difficulties in respect to labor, the way was prepared for the evolution of the labor argument—which is to be traced in the subsequent pages.

CHAPTER III

THE DEVELOPMENT OF THE LABOR ARGUMENT TO 1824.

Having concluded the survey of the fundamental facts and conditions upon which the argument was based, let us turn to the development which the argument itself underwent at the hands of protectionists. The attitude of their opponents and the changing character of their position must likewise be considered in order to enable us to understand and to explain the evolution of the labor argument for protection.

In the preliminary tariff struggle of 1816 the subject of labor was given little attention, except in relation to that of women and children and of persons who would probably not give all of their time to other industries. Protection to cotton, however, served to accentuate this phase of labor. The demoralization of this industry was a heavy blow to progress in manufacturing enterprises. The quasi-protection which it had received during the long period of political turmoil in Europe having been suddenly withdrawn, it was forced to fall back upon its inherent power to maintain itself. The rapid advancement which the introduction of machinery had afforded gave strength to the cotton industry, and the preponderance of women and children in the mills, together with the comparatively low wages paid them, also operated in its favor. The employment of this labor having been permitted, and having risen to considerable proportions, it became difficult to permit the collapse of this industry, not only for the sake of the capital invested, but also on account of the fact that the labor employed was the least independent. Protectionists scored a victory at a point where opposition was apt to be least concentrated and persistent, but it opened the way for the advent of an entire protective system. The apparent advantage in securing and continuing a form of labor unfitted for agricultural pursuits, and which would not be drawn from that industry, was very great. General sentiment favored economic development. The idea of restriction had little root, and protection to cotton was not regarded as a purely restrictive measure.

Although Calhoun and others had defended the manufacturing system, the subject was still unsettled and strong opposition continued to appear. The system was denounced as intrinsically injurious and pernicious in its effect. The agricultural and commercial interests were politically the more powerful and were reluctant to permit the introduction of a third claimant. The nature of this opposition is aptly expressed in the following extract from a speech delivered in Congress in 1821.[1] "It is not to be wondered at that the advocates for the supremacy of the General Government should defend a policy which is calculated to aggrandize it by creating a new class of dependents, but it is greatly to be wondered at that the friends of States' Rights should ever have defended it. It can only be because they have not fully perceived its certain consequence. It is believed that no candid mind can fail to perceive that the effect of the manufacturing and its kindred systems will be to transfer a great portion of the wealth of the agriculturists to the other classes. If wealth is thus transferred so are the means of education, of knowledge, and consequently of power. The great influence which the manufacturers, scattered as they will be over the whole face of the country, must acquire will leave the agriculturists little hope that if they once assent to their system it will ever be revoked. Among the means by which their influence in the government must be increased, the facility which they must derive from our popular modes of election, of directing the suffrages of the persons they employ, is not the least worthy of consideration. This apprehension is not diminished by the consideration that their dependents, as we are told, will consist principally of foreigners. Nor is it desirable to undersell foreign manufacturers; for in order to do so, we must not

---

[1] *Ann. of Cong.*, 37: 1678-79.

only equal them in skill, machinery, ingenuity, industry, etc., but we must equal them in human degradation and wretchedness. We must drive our laborers from the fields to those dismal and demoralizing abodes where they sink into hopeless stupidity and penury; where health and morals frequently become victims to hard labor and to the laws of poverty and hunger.''

Closely akin to this view was that of Barbour of Virginia,[2] who claimed that the manufacturer has no source of revenue but his labor, which he must constantly sell to a master; that not his own will but the will of his master was the rule of his conduct; that his condition was one of servility while that of the agriculturist is one of independence; and that physically the former is inferior. He argued that the interests of agriculture are identified with those of the community, while those of the manufacturer are not. Why should a class be created in society whose interests are opposed to those of the rest of society? We should not imitate Europe. Because she has been successful in manufacturing enterprise is no reason why we, with our comparatively sparse population, should attempt to follow a similar course.

These opinions are but typical expressions of the views of those who persistently opposed the introduction of the factory system. Others continued to argue along similar lines. In 1831 the popular demonstrations in favor of protection were, rightly or wrongly, ascribed to undue influence exerted by protectionists, while the condition of the operatives at Lowell and elsewhere was made the subject of attacks upon the manufacturing system.

Two main objections thus appear against manufacturing: first, the possibility that its development would eventually cause the political subordination of agriculture and of commerce. In this field of activity it was not to be trusted and it would attempt to tear down the original industries of the nation. It was feared that the laborers would be dependent upon the master manufacturer to such an extent that their political connections would also reflect their employer's views instead of their

---

[2] *Abridgement of Debates of Congress,* 6: 637.

own. It was claimed that the men would be driven to the polls and forced to vote in obedience to the wishes of their masters, and that their political independence would be sacrificed.

The other objection was based on moral grounds. This was urged at the very outset even before the factory system was established. In 1803 artisans and manufacturers of Philadelphia were sufficiently agitated over the charge that manufacturing industry was a breeder of vice vigorously to deny it in their petition to Congress. Furthermore they pointed to conditions in Europe where, according to their claim, crime was far more prevalent in commercial than in manufacturing towns. Protectionists defended the condition of the factory girls and attempted to minimize its disagreeable and unwholesome features. Placed upon the defensive, they refused to concede the disadvantages of the factory system. Again in 1827 the secretary of the treasury denied that rational moral grounds for objections to manufactures existed, nor would he admit that they led to physical deterioration.[3] Pointing to Europe he said that the most enlightened, opulent, and powerful nations there had the greatest proportion of manufacturers to other classes, and that those countries having an undue predominance of agricultural population were the poorest.

The struggle against the factory system on these grounds virtually ceased before 1830 and no important objections to the natural growth of manufactures were urged. Economic conditions were forcing a rapid development of this industry, and the formation of a laboring class could not be prevented. It became useless to struggle against it. The best that could be hoped for was the prevention of an unnatural increase of this class by removing the artificial stimulations to industry. Other grounds than moral and political objections then necessarily became the bases of the more effective lines of argument against the protective tariff.

From the very beginning of the tariff controversies the fact of high wages gave the protectionists a vast amount of trouble. They had attempted to meet the difficulty and still continued

---

[3] *Report on Finance, 1815-28,* 390.

in part to do so by urging the advisability of employing other than the ordinary labor engaged in the principal industries. This, however, did not suffice, and it became necessary to meet directly the contention that the wages of American labor were so high that our capital could not compete with that of foreign countries. Some of the objections, for example, made by free-traders to the system were enumerated by Matthew Carey as follows:[4]

The demoralizing effects of manufactures.
Injurious interference with commerce.
High rate of wages.
Vacant lands ought first to be settled.

In refutation of the claim that the price of labor was too high to permit successful manufacturing in the United States, he urged several important considerations: first, that numerous branches of manufacturing, in which manual labor alone was employed, had in consequence of public patronage arrived at perfection and prospered for many years; e. g., hats, boots, shoes, paper, books, etc. Of these products more than three-fourths of our consumption was supplied by the American manufacturer. Second, that even if labor were dear the objection would not apply to industries which employed considerable machinery, especially when the cheapness and advantage of our water power is given due weight. Third, that those industries employing the most machinery, aided by cheap labor and differing least from industries abroad needed protection. Finally, that the wages paid in England were, in many branches of industry, as high as those in America. In this connection he showed that the average wages of journeymen artisans and manufacturers in London were rated at thirty shillings per week, in other English towns at twenty-six shillings, and that boys of ten years and girls from twelve to fourteen years could almost maintain themselves. On the other hand, he pointed to the general unemployment of the period, to the fact that large numbers of people were at that time, (1821), working for their board alone, and to the enormous increase of paupers in New York and Philadelphia.

---
[4] Carey, M., *Essays on Political Economy*, 430 ff.

These were formidable objections to the high-wage argument of the free-trader, but they were exceptionally strong and effective during the years of depression and up to the year 1824 when the tariff was revised in favor of protection. During the tariff debate of 1820 perhaps the greatest objection to protection, as far as the laboring classes were concerned, was based on the moral and political grounds of opposition already mentioned. The high price of labor was made less prominent than in prosperous times although protectionists were given both horns of the dilemma; that if wages were not higher here than abroad there was no need of protection, and if they were higher, then other industries must be more profitable.

By 1824 the tariff question had become more prominent. The West was solidly in favor of protection. The agricultural interests favored it, because they were searching for a market for their products, and the home-market argument was the strongest one that could be urged. The South had become strongly free-trade in sentiment, and believed that protection was a device to enrich the North at her expense. New England was almost evenly divided, the anti-tariff men having a small majority. New York and Pennsylvania were quite solidly for protection.

The importance of labor now began to assume greater proportions, as is natural with the increase of the laboring class. The high wages paid to labor again became the subject of heated controversy. An increase of the duty on iron was one of the objects that protectionists sought. Fuller of Masschusetts, in discussing this feature of the proposed bill, claimed that in the manufacture of iron our greatest expense was for labor, that no improved machinery could be made serviceable as a substitute for labor, and that for a century to come the population of our country could not reach such a state of redundancy as materially to reduce the rate of wages.[5] Consequently success in manufacturing enterprise would be entirely out of the question.

McDuffie of South Carolina, who continued to figure for two decades in tariff debates, argued that, "In all those manufactures which principally result from manual labor; such, for example,

---
[5] *Ann. of Cong.*, **42:** 1706.

as iron—the high price of labor here, which is the most conclusive evidence of our prosperity, renders it impossible that we can maintain a competition with foreigners."[6] Our machinery, he said, was inferior; our capital dearer; and our experiment in the cotton industry gave little evidence of the value of protection. He made sport of the alleged unemployment which his opponents claimed prevailed in many parts of the country. All the idlers needed to do was to "go to work." It was ridiculous to speak of wages at 12½ cents per day. Even in the poorest portions of the country, he would guarantee at least 50 cents per day. It was not distress but discontent which troubled our people. "The admitted fact that a common laborer in this country receives double the wages that a common laborer in the most favored nation of Europe receives, and labors little more than half the time, conclusively demonstrates the impolicy of protecting by duties those manufactures of the price of which labor is the principal constituent."

Webster, at that time the chief representative of the commercial interests of New England, in a powerful speech on the tariff touched the same subject. Speaking of the alleged existence of idle hands, he said, "The price of labor is a conclusive and unanswerable argument to the idea. It is known to be higher with us than in any other civilized state and this is the greatest proof of all proofs of general happiness."[7] Repiying to the statement that Swedish serfs make iron for us at seven cents a day, he asked whether we had any labor in this country that could not be better employed than in a business which did not yield the laborer more than seven cents a day. The real question was, could we produce the article in a useful state at the same cost or nearly so. The manufacture of iron was an unproductive business and we were not poor enough to be obliged to follow it. It would cost us precisely what we could least afford; that is, great labor. The manual labor of a country was limited and could not be suddenly increased. Machinery would do something to supply the deficiency but it was quite inadequate. Should we buy this iron and let our laborers

---

[6] *Ibid.*, 2407 ff.
[7] *Ibid.*, 2062 ff.

earn their greater reward or employ our labor in this line and tax the consumer for the loss sustained? In this speech, Webster struck deeply into the heart of the protection argument. He pointed out the economic difficulties in the way of successful manufacturing, and indicated the gain which would result from a free-trade policy.

Barbour spoke in a similar vein and declared that our high wages showed that other pursuits than the iron industry were more profitable if manufactures were unable to pay that rate. High wages, if business continued, meant prosperity; for laborers were in the majority.

An argument of a slightly different nature was that urged by Rankin.[8] He opposed protection to manufactures, one of his objections being the injury that would be inflicted on laborers in other industries. He said there were 40,000 seamen, and that the shipwrights, boat builders, sail makers, chandlers, etc., whose labor depended upon prosperity in commerce numbered 250,000 or 290,000 in all. The interests of these men were at stake. The new system, even according to the speaker and with its possibilities greatly exaggerated, would not employ more than 500,000 men. Besides this a loss of $7,000,000 of revenue would be incurred. Then addressing himself to the causes which determine the rate of wages, he added: "The price of labor is governed by the price for which the inferior soil can be cultivated, where they are compelled to cultivate such soil. The American farmer can, with the same labor, grow more grain than the farmer of any other nation. He can better afford to pay from 20 to 50 per cent. on goods of foreign manufacture than have his attention directed from agriculture to domestic manufactures. This state of things will pass away, when our population becomes too dense to be supported by the cultivation of the best soil, and to be employed in commerce. Whenever that period arrives, we are then and not until then prepared for manufacturing."

Williams of North Carolina and Poinsett both pointed to the condition of the English laborer.[9] The effects upon him of

---
[8] *Ibid.*, 2010 ff.
[9] *Ibid.*, 2115, 2247.

manufacturing were extremely deplorable. Laborers worked from 14 to 17 hours per day. Wages were low, and when the laborers were thrown out of employment it was difficult to secure work again owing to the division of labor which prevailed and fitted a man for one kind of work only. The laborers were limited to a vegetable diet and extremes of wealth and of poverty were being produced by England's tariff laws. The poor, not the rich should be protected!

The contest was not confined to Congress, but the tariff was discussed by newspapers, publicists, merchants, manufacturers, and academic men. In argument and theory, however, they did not differ from the discussions in Congress. Thomas Cooper of South Carolina was one of the most ardent opponents of protection. On several occasions he wrote exhaustive economic discussions of the tariff question and replied in full vigor to the protectionist arguments based on high wages and unemployment.

Turning to the protectionist side of the controversy, we find that the argument in respect to labor is again emphasized and along lines similar to those advocated in previous tariff debates. Matthew Carey, as we have seen, denied the existence of high wages or tried to minimize their effect, but he did not favor a reduction of wages. However, there were those who saw in the lower prices for land and labor during the period of great depression, a greater opportunity for manufacturing industry to secure a foothold. The incentive to migrate westward was less while wages were at a lower level and more nearly within the ability of the manufacturers to pay.

Industry had rallied since the years 1819–20. Prices were better, and wages had risen again, but those of argicultural labor had gained very slowly. A writer[10] in 1825 declared that the farmers and their laborers had been for years in a state of ruin and misery; only a single year had elapsed since they began to emerge from this state; and that the wages of the agricultural laborer were yet little more than half those of manufacturing laborers. Conditions were not uniform throughout the coun-

---

[10] *Blackwood's Magazine,* May, 1825.

try. Transportation facilities were poor, and the immobility of labor and capital made distress possible in parts of the country while prosperity abounded elsewhere. Manufactures had made rapid progress in certain sections. The industry was growing rapidly in New England and in some of the middle states, especially Pennsylvania. Small plants too had been established in many parts of the West, thus furnishing a small home market for the farmer. But this was insufficient, and the agricultural interests, clamoring for a home market by means of the establishment of domestic manufactures, stoutly stood for a higher tariff. It was these interests which carried the day and secured the passage of the act of 1824.

Clay was the most powerful representative of the West and of the home market idea, but had to face all points of controversy in the tariff question. He emphasized the distress and prevailing hard times, especially those undergone by the people of the West, and lamented their misfortunes. In answer to the high wages argument usually made by free-traders, he replied: "The alleged fact of high wages is not admitted. The truth is, no class of society suffers more in the present stagnation of business than the laboring class. That is a necessary effect of the depression of agriculture, the principal business of the community. The wages of able bodied men vary from $5 to $8 per month, and such has been the want of employment in some parts of the Union, that instances have not been infrequent of men working merely for the means of present subsistence. If the fact were true that the wages of labor are high, I deny the correctness of the argument founded upon it. The argument assumes that natural labor is the principal element in the business of manufacturing. Inventions and machinery have produced a new era in the last few years."[11] He admitted that formerly the argument had great weight, but with the tremendous advance in the line of new machinery, labor had lost its former importance as an item of cost. Therefore the contention of his opponents had little value at the present time.

Wood of New York claimed that hands in sufficient number could be found to fill the establishments that would be erected

---

[11] *Ann. of Cong.*, **42:** 1973.

for some time to come, and that the number would increase as they would be required for new employment.[12] In addition to this expression of optimism, however, he argued that the price of labor was relative, that it must be considered in proportion to the compensation obtained for other employments, and that the advent of machinery had done away with most of the difference. The additional price of goods would, on the other hand, not be an advantage for the manufacturer merely. The farmer would get part of the benefit in higher prices for the raw material, the laborer in higher wages and the manufacturer would get ordinary profits only.

Even Benton, from beyond the Mississippi—a friend of the home market idea—urged the development of manufactures and saw no danger in it for the American workingman.[13] Clay had in 1820 spoken of the disinclination of many to emigrate to the West, and of the field this fact offered in the East for manufacturing industry. Benton's argument differed from this but had a similar end in view. He contended that too large a proportion of our population was employed in agriculture; that a surplus of agricultural products existed; that no market for these goods was forthcoming; that manufacturing had advantages here; and that attending circumstances were such as to save us from the demoralizing effects occasioned by similar establishments elsewhere. In other words, Benton pointed out the need of the growth of a manufacturing population, or laboring class, but depreciated the moral degradation which the opponents of protection asserted would necessarily accompany an extensive manufacturing system. On the other hand, eastern men quite naturally and logically exaggerated the disadvantages of migration to the wilderness, while hoping for the establishment of a manufacturing system to prevent the continued exodus from the East.

Protectionists furthermore emphasized the argument of unemployment wherever possible. The affected regions were wont to place stress upon this point. Factory districts which had not yet completely recovered cried out for aid. The tariff men of

---

[12] *Ibid.*, 2081.
[13] *Ibid.*, **41:** 693.

Philadelphia again pointed out the need of protection, after calling attention to closed factories and unemployed labor. Weavers in New York protested against the importation of British goods, and the mechanics of the larger cities demanded a greater degree of protection.[14]

The foregoing brief review of the principal arguments made in 1824 and previously in relation to the labor side of the tariff controversy, will serve to indicate the general nature of the problem, the economic conditions which obtained, and the points of departure for the subsequent development of the positions of the contending parties. It should be noted that free-traders had elaborated the following arguments:

1. The high wages paid in America preclude success in manufacturing industry.

2. The rate of wages is determined by the possible earnings of our western lands.

3. The application of highly paid labor to manufactures is an added cost to the consumer.

4. Our deficiency in machinery is too great a disadvantage to justify protective measures.

5. With the increase of population, according to the principles of Malthusianism, wages will eventually decline and then manufacturing can be successfully carried on.

6. The factory life of English workmen has made them a menace morally and politically, has injured them physically, and caused them to lead a wretched existence. America should not desire the addition of a similar population.

7. The interests of laborers in other industries should not be sacrificed in order to introduce a new industry.

8. The West offers a more inviting and profitable field for our workmen and as long as vacant lands exist the idea of considerable unemployment is absurd. There is, or can be, no large idle population.

On the other hand the contentions of protectionists may be briefly summarized under the following heads:

1. Manufacturing industry can secure considerable labor force

---

[14] McMaster, *History of the People of the United States*, 5: 85.

through the employment of women, children, and such labor as can turn from its regular employment during periods of intermission. This argument was urged by Hamilton, Matthew Carey and others.

2. The rate of wages in America is not so high as is commonly assumed. When compared with that of Great Britain, the difference is not so great.

3. Our rapid advancement in the perfection of machinery minimizes the influence of high wages.

4. A large number of American workmen are out of employment. A higher tariff would secure work for them.

5. Manufactures would give employment to persons who disliked to migrate westward.

6. A large number of foreign immigrants, possessing skill of various sorts, would be attracted to our shores, and they would assist in developing and diversifying American industry.

7. The transition of labor from agriculture to manufacturing would increase our home market and enhance our general prosperity.

CHAPTER IV

THE DEVELOPMENT OF THE LABOR ARGUMENT AFTER 1824

The early protection period was preeminently the one during which protection to capital was both the actual and ostensible purpose of tariff legislation. Labor interests were involved but they influenced the current of events very little. They were passive factors subject to legislation, not active forces determining it. The tariff discussions ending with the Compromise of 1833, which concluded active controversy for a period, however, gave increasing attention to this phase of the subject.

Toward the close of the third decade of the century the public land question became increasingly involved in our tariff discussions. The Foote Resolution was an incident showing the connection between the two problems. The struggle of the western states for economic and political power had important bearings. Their increasing fight for preemption laws and a reduction in the price of lands was a significant fact. The West grew with tremendous rapidity, however, before these favors were granted; and drew a large part of its rapidly increasing population from New England and other eastern states. The latter were compelled to content themselves with a comparatively slow growth and they began to see the dawn of a new era when political predominance should be wrested from them and placed in the hands of the states of the West. Manufactures had made remarkable strides in the East, still the opportunities of the West lured men away. The labor supply was deserting the factory for the farm. The eastern states were quite solidly opposed to the legislation in respect to public lands favored by the western states. The latter were gaining too fast in population. By 1820 Ohio had outstripped Massachusetts. During the following decade the North Atlantic states gained 27.5 per cent. but the North Central states 86.5 per cent. The New England states and New Jersey were slowly lagging behind. The South Atlantic states likewise were growing slowly. Hence to prevent the eastern states from becoming eclipsed, it was found necessary for them to hold their population. The manufacturing states believed the tariff would accomplish this end.

No one has stated this position more frankly than the ardent protectionist, Mr. Rush, Secretary of the Treasury, whom we have already quoted. In his Annual Report (1827) he says:[1] "The ratio of capital to population should if possible be kept on the increase. When this takes place the demand and compensation for labor will be proportionately increased and the condition of the numerous classes of the community become improved. . . . The manner in which the remote lands of the United States are selling and settling, whilst it may possibly tend to increase more quickly the aggregate population of the country and the mere means of subsistence, does not increase capital in the same proportion. The creation of capital is retarded rather than accelerated by the diffusion of a thin population over a great surface of soil. The further encouragement of manufactures by legislative means would be but a counterbalance and at most a partial one to the encouragement of agriculture by legislative means, standing out in the very terms upon which the public lands are sold."

As august a body of men as those composing the Convention of Friends of American Industry held at New York in 1831 dared to give expression to similar sentiments. In their memorial[2] to Congress they expressly stated that the establishment of domestic manufactures had the effect of restraining emigration from the settled to the unsettled parts of the country; that a protective policy would enable men to invest their capital and labor in manufactures at home instead of being compelled to

---

[1] *Report on Finance*, 1815-28, 405.
[2] *Cong. Debates*, 8: Appendix, 126.

emigrate and to occupy themselves in clearing land; that the tide of emigration would be checked throughout the settled parts of the Union and the population become more consolidated. At the same time they declared themselves as not opposed to the growth and prosperity of the West, and that the pursuit of agriculture alone was not conducive to the greatest prosperity. Besides there were other disadvantages to the people of the western states if their industry should remain undiversified. The same ideas took form and received expression in Congress itself. The real animus of the argument, however, was more hostile to the West than appears upon the surface.

The dispersion of our population was regarded as mischievous because it tended to weaken the East and add to the growth and power of the West. A protective policy which would equalize conditions so as to enable the eastern manufacturer to pay the wages demanded by the laborer, who would otherwise go West, received the strong adherence of the states principally affected. No wonder then that eastern protectionists were largely opposed to a liberal land policy, and that the latter drew upon the freetraders for much of the support it received.

This effort to swell the laboring population of the manufacturing states so as to permit the rapid growth of industry there, aroused the anger of western men. Anxious to develop their states, they looked with disfavor upon the retardation of emigration. Benton, who in 1824 had made an appeal for the laboring classes; who had stated that the laborer should receive a reasonable price for his labor and be enabled to procure the comforts of life and to educate his family; and who had conceded the disinclination of many to migrate to the unsettled portions of the country, now attacked the motives and principles of the protectionists who uttered sentiments such as those expressed above. He was opposed to methods which would prevent the free development of the West. Benton's attitude was a typical one, and western men, although the majority still remained protectionists, began to analyze the sectional aspects of the tariff question more closely. They were especially concerned with the disposal of our labor supply and while eastern manufacturers were desirous of retaining it, the western men, on the other hand, were anxious to attract it to the fertile lands of the new states.

The intrusion of this phase of the tariff controversy indicates in a measure the straits in which manufacturers found themselves at the time of the tariff of 1828 and 1832. Many of them were under the necessity of reducing wages or shutting down their establishments unless timely protective duties came to their support. This pressure, in part, intensified opposition to western emigration, for the latter only accentuated the difficulties.

The arguments for and against protection continued to develop along the lines already indicated, although signs of change began to appear. The hope of protectionists that their policy would continue to attract immigrants still possessed vitality. Madison believed this to be a strong point and expressed himself to that effect. After declaring that protection called labor from the more to the less profitable industry, he remarked: "It loses that character in proportion to the effect of the encouragement of attracting skillful laborers from abroad. Something of this kind has already taken place among ourselves and much more of it is in prospect. It appears, indeed, from the general history of manufacturing industry, that the prompt and successful introduction of it in new situations has been the result of emigrating from countries in which manufactures had gradually grown up to a prosperous state."[3] He then instanced the migration from Greece to Italy, from Italy to Spain, and from Flanders to England as proofs of his assertion. Even the Free-trade Convention of 1831 spoke of "the inducement it (protection) may have afforded to some skillful artists and operatives to emigrate."

Protectionists resented the term "restrictionists" applied to them, and naturally so when one considers their attempt to utilize a greater labor force than would otherwise be employed. In this connection the results which the textile industries secured

---

[3] Letter of Madison to Jos. C. Cabell, Oct. 30, 1828. See *Free-Trade Advocate*, 1: 39-40.

were still advanced as weighty arguments. The Free-trade Convention was forced to take cognizance of this fact also and in its memorial said:[4] "We are told . . . that the restrictive system is intended to bring into action a quantity of labor beyond what was previously actually put forth. That immediately employed in the protected branches is shown, by the result, to be on the contrary generally less productive than if applied to other pursuits. Yet there is an exception, which in some branches seems to alleviate the evil. The female labor employed in the cotton and woolen manufactures, appears from the rate of their wages to be more productive than if applied to the ordinary occupations of women."

The special attention given to the subject of wool and woolens by Congress and the country at large in 1827, 1828, and 1832; and the difficulties which many cotton and woolen manufactories experienced, continued to place emphasis upon the employment of women. Frequent charges, however, were made against this class of labor. Its weak points were constantly subjected to attack. Home was said to be the place for the "tender female." Girls should find employment in the dairy, kitchen, or on the farm. Factory life was uncertain. The operatives may be suddenly turned out of employment. The girls were held under strict subordination and helplessness. Arguments of this kind were indefinitely multiplied and had to be met by counter assertions from friends of manufacturing industry.[5] The bright side of life at Lowell, indeed, made a profound impression. Foreigners such as Harriet Martineau, William Scoresby, and even Charles Dickens, who visited the mills, gave favorable accounts of our factory life. President Jackson, who was invited to Lowell, found it in gala attire and went away well pleased. The dark side, however, was a menacing one and the struggle of the cotton operatives was one of the incipient moves of American labor for a higher standard of life. This was to be reflected presently in the new turn which our tariff discussions began to take.

[4] *Memorial of the Free-Trade Convention*, 19.
[5] See: *Cong. Debates*, 8: 232; 407. *Free-Trade Advocate*, 1: 4; 2: 338, etc.

Free-traders continued to attack the argument on unemployment and to emphasize the high rate of wages. It was argued that wages would have fallen if many had been unemployed, but that wages were as high as formerly. Raguet admitted that there was some idleness in the cities where the new influx of foreigners was being felt.[6] Time was required to distribute them, and meanwhile some of them were idle. Employment at moderate wages, however, could always be secured on farms, turnpikes, and canals, while permanent want of employment could not exist when tens of millions of acres of fertile land could be had for $1.25 per acre. Agriculture could not be overdone. Any concession of idleness, however, gave the protectionists additional ground for their contentions.

During the period of 1827–1833 the causes determining the wages of labor were more carefully analyzed, the effect of protection upon the rate of wages was discussed, and the interests of the consumer were emphasized. In discussing the wages of workmen, one writer says: "Tariffs and monopolies cannot help them since their wages are regulated by the average rates of other labor which they must have whether their employers make or lose."[7] The wage-earner is not benefited by the American system; the proprietors alone gather the advantage. Here we have pointed out the relation between the labor engaged in different professions and the cause of an average rate of wages. Barbour in 1824 had clearly indicated the primary cause determining wages in America, but he overlooked the accidental elements or disturbing factors which protectionists emphasized. Gallatin, seven years later, went a step further and said: "Wages are one of the elements of the price of commodities, and if higher in a country which nevertheless affords certain commodities at a less price than the country where the wages are lower, there must be a difference in climate, soil, skill, or some other circumstance which produces that result. But in each country the price is determined either by its productive-

---

[6] *Free-Trade Advocate*, 1: 3. Jan. 3, 1829.
[7] *Report of a Committee of the Citizens of Boston and Vicinity opposed to a Further Increase of Duties on Importations*, 123. Boston. 1827.

ness or by the proportion between demand and supply in that country, and in no manner whatever by what may be that productiveness or that proportion in any other country, whether there is or there is not an intercourse between the two countries. . . . The price of labor is in each regulated exclusively by the respective proportion of supply and demand and the state of society."[8]

Strong as was this argument theoretically, it failed to meet the entire situation. In the East the labor problem was becoming an important one. It presented three phases. A large part of the factory operatives consisted of persons who would otherwise probably have remained unemployed, and, according to Newman, received a lower wage than the average paid to mechanics.[9] Again after 1830, immigration became more important, the number of foreigners entering that year being 23,322, while that for 1832 was 60,482, against only 10,199 in 1825. Lastly, the East was desirous of retaining its male manual labor force, but recognized the necessity of paying good wages in order to succeed in this attempt.

On the other hand, the low price of cotton between 1830 and 1840 increased the activity of the South against the tariff and caused it to examine more closely into the effect of protection upon the northern states. These facts tended to confuse the arguments of free-traders on wages and labor, especially when theories were abandoned and the concrete conditions were discussed. Consequently free-traders were not united as to the effect of protection on wages. John Bell,[10] in 1832, speaking of the South and Southwest said that these regions secured none of the benefits of protection either in higher wages or profits, but had to pay enhanced prices for the goods they bought from the tariff states. Another anti-tariff writer[11] (1828) said that a protective tariff had a necessary tendency to increase the price of labor generally, and also that of every article in proportion as it was the fruit of labor. Dew in maintaining that restriction

---
[8] *Memorial of Free-Trade Convention*, 1831, 31-2.
[9] Newman, S. P., *Elements of Political Economy*, 158.
[10] *Cong. Debates*, 8: 41.
[11] *The American System*. Nathan Hale's *Press*, 1828.

prevented a fall of profits and retarded emigration, really admitted that it increased the nominal wages of labor. McDuffie, in 1830, said that the price of labor had fallen in the South but in the North, including all pursuits, had advanced during the preceding thirty years. Two years later Hayne exclaimed, "How can protection diminish the cost of production? What are the elements of price? Are they not the cost of the raw material—the wages of labor—and the interest of capital, and how can these be lessened by a tax on the article?"[12] In fact he and many other southern men held that the North was securing an advantage in prosperity at the expense of the South, and that the high remuneration of northern labor was largely paid for indirectly by the southern people. Other free-traders held similar views, but those of the North adhered principally to the theories of Gallatin and those formerly held by Webster, who was now being quoted far and wide by the opponents of protection.

The interests of the laborer were being considered from the standpoint of the consumer, but to a comparatively small degree only from that of a separate class demanding attention. The effect of protection upon the consumer was the chief consideration employed by free-traders in reply to the protectionists' emphasis upon the importance of the interests of the producer. The phrase "taxing the many for the benefit of the few" was current from the beginning of active tariff controversy; so with the charge that protection increased prices. The term "laboring class" was used very loosely, but McDuffie in 1824, with more precision declared that the laboring class would be sacrificed for the benefit of the capitalists and that the question lay between those who produce more than they consume of the articles subject to duty and those who buy the surplus production.[13] Writers and speakers furthermore declared that the American system robbed the laboring classes for the benefit of the idle and taxed the poor for the benefit of the rich.[14] The

---

[12] *Cong. Debates*, 8: 92.
[13] *Ann. of Cong.*, 42: 2421.
[14] *Banner of the Constitution*, 2: 38 ff.

Free-trade Convention of 1831, however, less moved by demagogues or by the excesses of southern opinion, dispassionately discussed the question in the following manner: "It is clear that the mechanic who pays twenty dollars more for the implements of his trade, the necessary clothing of his family, and the sugar it consumes, must either enhance the price of the products of his industry in the same proportion, or receive so much less for his labor. The nominal wages, of the journeymen and of the laborer, do now remain the same, whilst the true price of their labor, the compensation they actually receive, has been lessened to an amount precisely equal to the enhanced price of the necessary articles they must purchase."[15]

The distinction between the real and nominal price of labor is clearly brought out in this extract and also the bearing of higher prices upon the wages of the labor not engaged in an industry receiving protection. On the other hand, coming from the laboring man himself, we have a severe arraignment of the protective system as then in operation. Writing to the chairman of a meeting of working men in Boston, Seth Luther, formerly a carpenter, said that manufacturers had called him spy, agitator, etc., that he had exposed the unrighteousness of those who imported foreign wool to reduce the price of wool to our farmers; foreign workmen to cut down the wages of American citizens; and foreign machinery to throw our own machinists out of employment; and who still pretended to support American industry.[16] Such sentiments were followed in 1837 by petitions from one thousand to two thousand of the laboring class and poor of Boston for a repeal of the duty on coal, and from the inhabitants of other towns for similar relief.[17] The Senate committee on manufactures in a report of that year admitted the high price of American labor but claimed in addition that the injustice and oppression of protection falls almost entirely upon the poorer classes. These facts and arguments are typical of this transition period. They show the in-

---
[15] *Memorial to Congress*, 49.
[16] *Address to Workingmen*, 4.
[17] *24th Cong., 2nd Sess.; Sen. Docs.*, 2: No. 102.

fluence of a one-sided southern opinion upon the labor phase of tariff controversy. The effect of agitation by tariff reformers of the North is likewise important and leads to a maturer consideration of the theoretical aspects of the question. The increasing importance of the laboring class in politics adds to the current confusion which is only to be cleared away by antagonism to the newly developing theory of protectionists in respect to pauper labor.

Turning now to the growth of protectionist doctrine after 1824, we find that an important evolution is taking place. Our manufacturers are still contending with certain disadvantages, among them, the high price of labor. Woolen manufacturers during 1827 and 1828 were especially discontented and asked for higher duties on woolen goods. The Harrisburg convention of the former year took the position that a nation whose labor was dear could not without ruin carry on commerce with one whose labor was cheap. Machine industry, however, was making rapid progress, and 10,020 patents were issued between 1790 and 1836. Under such conditions the more eager and optimistic protectionists agreed with Rush in his annual report of 1827 that: "The time has passed when objections might be made to manufactures from the limited amount of our population and the dearness of labor. Population in many parts of the Union is sufficient for any operations of manual labor, while science by applying its inventions to this kind of labor has abridged its expensiveness."[18] In Congress protectionists were wont to take a similar view. Young[19] of R. I. admitted that there were considerable differences in the case of the wages here and abroad of agriculturists, mechanics, sailors, etc., but that foremen and overseers were paid higher wages in England and that we employed proportionately more women and children. Moderate protectionists, such as Professor Newman of Bowdoin College, advanced the same argument and even the free-trader Raguet said that the wages paid to cotton and woolen employees could not be so high as that paid in certain other lines because less

---

[18] *Reports of Finance*, 1815-28, 399.
[19] *Cong. Debates*, 6: 900.

manual labor, skill, and intellect were required and the number of competitors would be greater. Everett and Davis of Massachusetts both began to minimize the wage difficulty but soon advanced to firmer ground. That the argument relative to the comparative dearness of American labor was not dead is evidenced by the fact that in 1837 free-traders still referred to it, and occasionally protectionists did likewise. As late as 1840 the anachronistic Governor Ellsworth of Connecticut declared that unless the eastern states could sustain themselves by their manufactures they were destined ere long to lose their importance; that he did not believe that wages could be much reduced even if attempts were made; that the laborers would otherwise go West; and finally that we had not really suffered from high prices and wages.

This species of argument had lost its weight by this time. Powerful as it had been once, it was always a negative argument as far as labor was concerned. It was urged to prove the need of protection to capital and offered nothing directly for the benefit of the laboring class. It is to the positive side of the labor argument therefore that attention must be turned in order to understand the growth and evolution of the later doctrine. The necessarily increasing concern for the laborer and the theories relating to him prompted the development which culminated in the present high wage doctrine.

Protectionists continued to exploit the subject of unemployment to a considerable extent.[20] In 1830 Raguet said, "The doctrine that there are in the United States a vast number of persons who can not procure employment has long been a favorite one with the restrictive party." Similarly he quoted Clay as claiming that protection was invaluable to the laboring classes because it increased and multiplied the demands for their industry and gave them an option of employments. Clay did, indeed, frequently refer to the subject of distress and later (1832) maintained that protection extended to almost every mechanical art. As a western man, however, he took the subject of labor less seriously.

[20] *Principles of Free-Trade*, 46.

Niles pointed out the supposed value of protection in the following words: "The nature and tendency of the American system is to encourage the laboring people, the free men and the free women of the United States, and by rendering the means of subsistence more certain to promote marriages, and to relieve the fear of the poor because of increase in their families."[21]

Young showed that wages for laborers on the wharves were as high in 1832 as in 1816, and maintained that the American system benefited northern labor. Sprague[22] in the same year argued that in every tariff adjustment, primary regard should be had for the interests of the laboring classes of the community and that two problems arose in that connection; first, the giving of employment to those who would be without it otherwise; second, the problem of how to make labor more productive and profitable. That system, he said, was best which gave to labor the greatest amount of comforts and conveniences. Robbins of Rhode Island[23] made an appeal for manufactures, claiming that they made a demand for labor and resulted in improving the condition of the laboring classes. Evans,[24] a New England congressman, devoted a large part of his speech to the subject of labor. Protectionists had become alive not only to the bright side, but also to the oppressions of English factory life. He said that these oppressions did not arise from protection but that this policy had fostered and encouraged our labor and industry. The laboring classes were the largest part of our population and the more they received the greater would be our prosperity. Denny of Pennsylvania claimed that the product of foreign labor thrown into our markets would impair our industry and deprive our laboring classes of the means of subsistence, or drive them into agriculture. Other eastern protectionists, such as Stewart and Davis, emphasized the subject of labor in 1832, but the character of their argument was more modern and will receive attention in a later chapter.

[21] *Niles' Register*, 35: 316.
[22] *Cong. Debates*, 8: 604.
[23] *Ibid.*, 493.
[24] *Ibid.*, 3422.

In 1831 a convention of protectionists was held at New York. In their address they declared that, "It is to rescue the labor of the American people from an inferiority—a subjection at once dishonorable and burdensome, at once degrading to its character while it increases its toils—that those very laws (protective) were originally passed, have all along continued and now exist. . . . It is thought to be a wise policy to multiply the inducements to apply capital to the employment of labor at home rather than to purchase abroad and traffic in commodities of foreign production, by which the capital of the country is made to set in motion foreign labor. The American system offers security and inducement to American capital and gives employment and vigor to American labor. Labor is not the mere instrument of capital but an intelligent, active principle. The stimulus to labor can be increased by applying capital to home production. We believe that while it benefits all, its highest recommendation is found in its beneficial action upon the many—the laboring classes—the working men. Our system tends directly to increase the effective power and remuneration of labor, thus multiplying the means, the comforts and enjoyments, of the laboring classes and raising them in the scale of civilization and social life."[25]

Webster as early as 1831 declared himself in favor of protection to labor, and pointed to the influence of mechanics in securing the adoption of the Constitution and its relation to protection. He began to appeal to mechanics to support the protective policy, and in 1833 he said, "Nothing can be worse than that laws concerning the daily labor and the daily bread of whole classes of the people should be subject to frequent and violent changes. A just and a leading object in the whole system is the encouragement and protection of American manual labor . . . "[26] At a later date he called attention to the protected workmen of Connecticut—those engaged in the hat, tinware, and woolen industries. The ends to be obtained by protection were to secure steady employment to brawny arms and indus-

---

[25] *New York Convention of Friends of Domestic Industry*, 7, 18 ff.
[26] Webster, *Works*, 1: 283.

trious hands. "The free labor of the United States deserves to be protected. The true way to protect the poor is to protect their labor."[27]

Men like Buchanan from states possessing industries affected by a reduction of duty, such as coal, iron, cotton, woolen, etc., began more and more to emphasize the subject of protection to labor. It was largely a question of maintaining men at their employment and the difficulties which would ensue, were protection withdrawn; while the comparison between the European and the American laborer and the probable degradation of the latter were more sparingly dwelt upon. The really important argument which protectionists had developed and exploited during the controversies of 1828, 1832–33 and 1837 was the increased employment at remunerative wages which protection would afford. Undeniably many eastern men desired to use protection as a means of preventing emigration and western men hoped to build up manufactures to strengthen their home market, but the general principle as stated above remains true. In addition it was continually claimed that protection did not raise prices because competition would force them down; that therefore the laborer did not suffer.

In the above chapter we have traced the evolution of the labor argument for, and that against, the protective tariff during the first protective period; we have pointed out the characteristic features of the argument and the underlying causes for the same; but we have omitted the discussion of the subject of pauper labor, which was already mentioned at this time. It was, however, not the typical nor characteristic argument of the period, and only received general attention later. Therefore we shall treat the early stages of its development in connection with the general evolution of the doctrine.

---

[27] *Cong. Debates*, 13: 1, 959-960.

CHAPTER V

FACTORS AFFECTING THE LABOR ARGUMENT

In order to understand more clearly the development of the pauper labor argument it is necessary to suggest briefly several facts and tendencies of this period of history. These in themselves are not closely connected with the tariff question, but indirectly they are largely responsible for the emergence of this phase of tariff discussion. Among these movements is the one which concerned itself with elevating the standard of life of the American workingman.

The debates in Congress between 1816 and 1825 show little sympathy for the aspirations of workingmen. The theory of Malthus influenced American statesmen to no inconsiderable extent. The problem, however, was not regarded as an imminent one, but the belief existed that wages would eventually decline. Rankin[1] in 1824, while contending that manufactures could not be successful, said, "This state of things will pass away when our population becomes too dense to be supported by the cultivation of the best soil, and to be employed in commerce. We are then and not until then prepared for manufacturing." Both protectionists and free-traders spoke of the time when wages would no longer be too high to prevent the development of industry. The following extract also indicates the point of view, "The high price of labor will be a barrier against home manufactures and the establishment of a general system of manufacturing would create a new demand for labor and increase the 'evil complained of.' "[2] The constant dissatisfaction

---
[1] *Ann. of Cong.*, 42: 2010.
[2] *New York American*, August 7, 1819.

with the "dearness of labor" reflects a wide-spread attitude, which changed, however, with the advent of the pauper labor argument. Although free-traders were charged in 1832 with holding that the natural price of wages was the mere subsistence of the laborer, many of them had begun to believe in the importance and dignity of labor. It must not be forgotten that the chief free-trade leaders were southern men, accustomed to an atmosphere of slavery. Occasionally invidious comparisons between free and slave labor were made. Protectionists, on the other hand, were forced by the laborers themselves to recognize the upward pressure of the masses.

Turning to the movement among workingmen, we find that considerable organization prevailed among journeymen mechanics before the tariff became a live issue in 1816. The conspiracy cases at New York, Philadelphia, and Pittsburg point clearly to this fact, and to the objects which labor intended to accomplish—higher wages and the employment of union men. In 1819 a writer refers to the "habit of associations among our workmen to enhance the price of labor."[3] The crisis of that year impaired the development of organization among the laboring men but by 1825 a self-conscious activity again strongly manifested itself.[4] Thousands moved to the West and the remainder struggled for greater advantages in the older states. An attachment to city life and the indisposition to emigrate restrained large numbers from leaving their old homes. The struggle now began to include a demand for a shorter work day. Various newspapers proclaimed the cause of the laborer and the *Mechanic's Free Press,* a labor publication conducted at Philadelphia between 1828 and 1831, did valiant service for the cause. The *Workingman's Advocate,* published in New York City from 1829 to 1835, also upheld the interests of labor.

The labor difficulties in the textile industries after 1828 materially affected the struggle for better conditions. In 1829 from 600 to 800 girls employed in a single cotton factory at Dover,

---
[3] *Ibid.*
[4] Ely, *Labor Movement in America,* 40.

New Hampshire, struck on account of stringent regulations.[5] They failed, but the lesson of cooperation was being taught. Strikes and combinations to prevent lower wages were common. The current of events is well illustrated by the view in respect to the social conditions of the time as expressed by a labor convention held at Boston in 1831. "The social evils arise from an illiberal opinion of the worth and rights of the laboring classes; an unjust estimation of their moral and intellectual powers; an unwise misapprehension of the effects which would result from the cultivation of their minds and the improvement of their condition; and an avaricious propensity to avail of their laborious services at the lowest possible rate of wages for which they can be induced to work."[6]

Whatever causes tended to depreciate the opportunities of the workingmen were held in disfavor. This accounts, in part, for the opposition to the Irish in New England. A large number of New York laborers feared that their wages would be reduced if 100,000 foreigners came to America annually.[7] The rapid improvements in machinery also tended to displace American workmen to some extent, and produced considerable discontent.[8] Seth Luther again voiced the opinions of this class of men, although the actual suffering from this cause was not great. An example of the attitude and purpose of the laboring classes is typified in the address to the public made by the working people of Manayunk, Pennsylvania, in 1833—a year which marks the beginning of a more vigorous trades' union movement.[9] They objected to a thirteen-hour day and opposed the attempts of employers to reduce their wages twenty per cent. because cotton had risen in value. They complained that their wages were barely sufficient to supply them with the necessaries of life, and that their children were as much oppressed as those of English factories. With reasonable hours and wages their children could be properly educated. The female workers, they asserted,

---

[5] *Free-Trade Advocate*, 2: 73-4.
[6] Casson, H. N., *Organized Self-help*, 144.
[7] Meyers, *Tammany Hall*, 159.
[8] Simpson, Stephen, *Working Man's Manual*, 133.
[9] *Examiner*, 1: 54-5.

were subject to the same burdens. Furthermore they desired to hear from the different trades' unions of the United States in regard to their regulations, etc.

The appeal to other trades' unions indicates a rising bond of sympathy among the laborers and the growth of concerted effort toward higher standards. In a similar way a Labor Convention at New York in 1834[10] resolved "that we recommend to the several Trades' Unions in the United States to oppose resolutely every attempt to reduce their wages, and to hold fast any additions they may receive." The great grievance of the unions, in fact, was said to be "inadequacy of wages," although they sometimes asked for a reduction of hours. Long hours and child labor, however, were important evils in the textile industries. Out of 57,000 persons employed in 12 states in cotton and woolen mills, 31,044 were, according to Luther, under 16 years of age, and 6,000 under 12. To relieve these grievances in addition to the others mentioned was no easy matter and largely accounts for the ceaseless struggles of the factory operatives. Measurable success here was attended by a general elevation in the standard of life.

The movement to secure higher wages was given additional momentum by a change of judicial attitude toward conspiracies. The customary decisions against the legality of conspiracies made it difficult for organized labor to secure even ordinary demands. Several decisions however, in 1836 in favor of the defendants in cases of this kind gave encouragement to the friends of labor, made organizations more effective, and aided the workingmen in their struggle for better conditions and higher wages.[11] This year marks the climax of the trades' union movement of the decade.

The increasing prosperity of the laboring classes was suddenly checked in 1837 by the obtrusion of a financial crisis. Short crops in 1836 and the paper inflation of the period had raised the prices of necessaries to stupendous figures.[12] Flour

---

[10] Potter, A., *Political Economy*, 264.
[11] *Philadelphia Public Ledger*, July 2, 1836.
[12] Parton, J., *Life of Jackson*, 312.

sold at $16.00 per barrel, and hardships were impending. Many manufacturers were compelled to dismiss some of their workmen, and large numbers of mechanics began to suffer from want. A mob in New York cried out for lower prices for bread, meat, rent, and fuel and then destroyed 1,000 bushels of wheat and several hundred barrels of flour.[13] The action of the Government in calling in gold and silver, together with the Specie Circular precipitated the crisis, and in a few months failure and distress were general. To what extent the prevailing low tariff was a contributory cause is uncertain, but many believed it to be a cause and seized upon this psychological moment to promote the interests of protection.

The growing distress suspended factories and mills and thousands of men were thrown out of employment, and enjoyed no means of subsistence. Many labor organizations collapsed and numbers of energetic men and women asked merely for help to secure work. Hundreds of laborers were dismissed from farms and country places in the fall of the year and found themselves without work.[14] In the early part of 1838 one-third of the 200,000 persons in New York City who subsisted by manual labor were said to have been wholly or partly out of employment.[15] Ten thousand persons were in utter poverty. Manufacturing, building, and business had enormously declined. The distress here and elsewhere continued for several years and was heavily felt in 1842. Pauperism was still so widespread that during the winter of 1841–42 it was estimated that from 30,000 to 50,000 people were destitute of the means of a week's comfortable existence, while the alms houses were full and overflowing.[16] The large number of mechanics and laboring men out of employment faced a gloomy future. Many of them migrated westward and others were desirous of going, but found it difficult to move. Many were not sufficiently informed concerning the West and had not the hardihood to go; at the same time depressed conditions from which relief was sought obtained

---

[13] *Niles' Register*, **51:** February 18, 1837.
[14] Greeley, *Recollections*, 144.
[15] *New Yorker*, January 20, 1838.
[16] *New York Tribune*, January 8, 1842.

there as elsewhere. The migration of Mormons from Missouri to Illinois, for example, was investigated and the conclusion drawn that "these people have no design to lower the wages of the laboring class but to procure something to save them from starving."[17] The attitude of the people, however, is no less plain, and certainly the competition of the unemployed had temporarily reduced wages.

The conditions in manufacturing industry were deplorable. Pennsylvania complained on account of the closing down of iron works and the unemployment which it occasioned. Manufacturers of leather, hats, and wares of various kinds were seriously affected. Many cotton mills,[18] says Bishop were about to close. They had several times reduced the wages of their operatives and were now waiting for Congress to revise the tariff. Other industries were disturbed and laborers dismissed from employment. Such conditions justified the Central Committee of Home Leagues in calling upon unemployed operatives to meet in their respective districts to consult together and devise means of relief. A new impulse was thus given to the protective tariff.

Manufacturing industry had now grown to considerable proportions in the United States. The number of persons employed in manufactures had risen by 1840 to 791,749. In the New England states the proportion engaged in this industry had risen from 21 per cent. in 1820 to 30.2 per cent. in 1840, and in the Middle states from 22.6 per cent. to 28 per cent. respectively. Furthermore these two divisions now employed 65.8 per cent. of the persons in the United States engaged in manufacturing and 52 per cent. of those occupied in mining. The total value of the product was $239,836,224 for manufacturing and $42,358,761 for mining.[19] In the former industry, New York, Massachusetts, and Pennsylvania led, while the latter state was easily the first in mining, iron and coal being the chief products. These facts show how important these industries were at this time in the eastern states, and what a blow commercial

---

[17] Bancroft, H. H., *History of Utah*, 137.
[18] *History of Manufactures*, 2: 421 ff.
[19] Tucker, George, *Progress of the United States*, 205 ff. Also *Census of 1840*.

depression was to the people of this section. Not all of the industries, it is true, were greatly depressed, but the rather general nature of the crisis operated to cause men to look to the tariff for a remedy even though the latter should act directly on certain industries only.

The growth of idealism and humanitarianism in America during this period of struggle for the laborer united with other movements to affect the new attitude toward labor and toward the protective tariff. Owen had begun his cooperative experiment in 1825. Labor stores were established, and agitators continued to inflame the workingmen. Their right to the whole product was asserted, and many of our eminent men were captivated by utopian schemes for social betterment, of which Brook Farm is an illustration. Horace Greeley, Albert Brisbane, George William Curtis were representatives of this movement. The old theology, on the other hand, tended to content men with their lot however humble, but the humanitarian movement began to emphasize the dignity of labor and the worth of man. William Ellery Channing typifies the new school in insisting upon the development of the individual.[20] He strongly advocated the elevation of all classes of citizens. In 1840 he pointed out the questionable effect of bringing the European laborer nearer to the American as improved steam navigation would assuredly do. He deplored the possibility of a competition which would depress the laboring classes of this country. Could our workmen stand their ground, he asked, against the half-famished, ignorant workman of Europe? Was there no danger that degradation such as that found among the overworked operatives of her factories and among her half-brutalized peasants would follow closer connections with Europe?

Other New England divines likewise stood for the elevation of the working classes. Philanthropy was gaining ground, and the intellectual and moral progress of the laborer received more attention. Such doctrines as these and the sympathy and aid of noted men of the hour naturally gave an additional impetus to the labor movement, and when these ideas took a political

---

[20] *Log Cabin*, July 18, 1840.

turn the relation between the tariff and the laborer became a subject of more extensive investigation and importance.

The immigration of foreign laborers and of many paupers began to cause some dissatisfaction. Massachusetts, in 1836, through its legislature asked Congress to pass a law to prevent immigration of foreign paupers. The municipal authorities of the large seaboard cities likewise called attention to the subject and Congress made an investigation in 1838. The committee in charge reported against the admission of paupers, vagrants and malefactors, and deprecated their blighting influence upon our population, especially upon the laboring classes. The question was not yet a sufficiently serious one and nothing was done. In 1842, however, the *New York Tribune* maintained that on account of immigration the supply of manual labor in that city would probably exceed the demand, and the price of labor compared with the cost of living would consequently be lower than in the rest of the country.[21] Immigration, on the contrary, could not glut the market and depress wages, as was popularly imagined, so long as the tariff was so adjusted as to preserve a proper proportion of manufacturing to agricultural labor, although at the points of disembarkation a temporary glut might be occasioned. Such utterances indicate the existence of local aggravation and show how opposition to the foreigner could take the less objectionable, although less logical, form of a demand for higher duties upon the products of foreign labor. Seth Luther had more boldly objected to immigration on the ground that this was the proper way of protecting American labor, but views of this kind were not extensively proclaimed.

The economic advancement of the working classes found its parallel in their increased political activity. Before 1828 the laborer was not considered an important factor in politics, although Tammany had made occasional concessions to secure his vote. In 1827 a workingmen's party originated in Philadelphia, and it polled a considerable number of votes besides securing the election of a number of its candidates but the movement subsided in 1830. A large number of workingmen

---

[21] *New York Tribune,* July 23, 1842.

[258]

had begun to realize that many reforms were needed for the elevation of their class and that their interests were receiving but little attention. An adequate system of public education, mechanic's lien laws, and other measures were advocated. A class consciousness had arisen and a difference of interests between master and journeyman mechanics was recognized. It was resolved to gain the reforms by embarking in politics on an independent basis, but the shrewd machinations of old political leaders eventually disrupted the new party, although not without concessions on their part.

In 1829 the workingmen organized a party in New York City,[22] the demand for a mechanic's lien law having failed. Matthew Carey's efforts in favor of the seamstresses had likewise stirred the laborers, who appointed a committee to investigate the condition of the industrial classes. The complaint became current that while the laborer remained poor his master was becoming rich. The new party met with some success and soon both Whigs and Democrats began to develop interest in the workingmen. In 1830 a Clay Workingman's Ticket, which favored a protective tariff, was nominated, while Tammany stood ostensibly for the cause of democracy.[23] The movement spread to various cities. In Baltimore the workingmen nominated candidates for members of the state legislature in 1833, while in Boston they pledged themselves to vote only for men favoring their measures of reform.[24] The independent movement, however, lacked stability and permanence. It was short-lived although occasional outbreaks continued to occur. But it had not failed. It forced the regular parties to give attention to both the laborers' votes and policies.

The Democratic party absorbed the larger part of this vote and the heavy support received by Jackson in the eastern states is largely due to the favorable attitude of mechanics and workingmen. The laboring classes in fact forced that party to indorse and support many of its measures. The Democrats catered

---

[22] McNeill, G., *Labor Movement*, 75.
[23] Meyers, *Tammany Hall*, 97-9.
[24] *Niles' Register*. 45: 49

less to property than did the Whigs, and thus naturally found more favor among the working classes. But elections can not be won without votes—a bit of wisdom which the Whigs soon realized. Bancroft, the historian, thought the day for the multitude had come, that the mechanic and the yeomanry were now to lead the march of progress. They had indeed made themselves heard and given new direction to economic and political tendencies.

The advent of the laborer in politics created new political turmoil. Laborers in mass meeting indorsed or disapproved of candidates for office. The friendship of Van Buren was distrusted. During the campaign of 1840 he was forced to reply to questions concerning his attitude toward the protective tariff and a reduction of the standard of wages. He had inaugurated the ten-hour day in Government establishments, yet laborers were dissatisfied, and he was made the scape goat for the prevailing ills and depression. The debate on the sub-treasury and on hard money in 1839–40 plainly indicates the rising importance of the laboring class. In 1824 such arguments as were now made would have been absurd. The adoption of the system, it was claimed, would reduce the wages of the laborer, and bring him to the level of his foreign competitors. The emphasis placed by its Whig opponents upon this cause for opposition is both significant and comprehensible. The resemblance between this argument and the labor argument for protection in 1842 is another striking fact. Harrison, on the other hand, was hailed as the "Poor Man's Friend" and the Whigs appealed to all classes of society. Charges against the aristocratic proclivities of the leaders of opposite parties were common and were weapons employed to capture the labor vote. The conversion of laboring men from one party to another was given adequate newspaper notice, while their views and arguments were used to best effect. The political importance of the workingmen was distinctly recognized, a fact which necessarily affected the public and ostensible position of each party on the leading questions of the day.

A number of considerations therefore arose which contributed vitally to the growing importance of the high wage argument for protection. The rapidly rising standard of life of the American workmen was gaining a momentum which could not be resisted. A rise of wages, not a diminution in the price of labor, was coming to be regarded as the just and permanent hope of the laborer. The social movements of the hour gave impetus to the struggle of labor. The effect of immigration upon the laborer was viewed with some alarm. The political activity of the working classes roused the old parties from their lethargy and called forth their reluctant attention to current social problems. Mechanics and workingmen held legislators to a more rigid accountability. The relation between new legislation and their own interests was extensively studied. The crisis of 1837 gave new cause for complaint and the popular preference for higher levels of prices was reflected in the opposition to a reduction of the nominal wages, entirely apart from the effect on its purchasing power. The struggle of the East against the West to retain its economic prestige necessitated new concessions to the workingmen. Finally the existence of slavery served to strengthen the defense of the wage system. The parallel growth of these movements and the political tension which they produced profoundly affected the discussion of the tariff. The older attitude could no longer be maintained, and the argument on the subject was therefore co-ordinated with the new ideas, ideals and conditions which obtained. The years 1841–42 seemed to be the culmination of the tendencies to which we have referred. Consequently a new importance was given to the pauper labor argument, the development and growth of which will be traced in the ensuing chapter.

CHAPTER VI

THE RISE OF THE PAUPER LABOR ARGUMENT

In tracing the labor argument in respect to the protective tariff, we have noticed several lines of development: First, protection afforded the advantage of adding to our available labor supply in manufacturing industry. This argument declined in importance with the growth of the factory system and the increase of immigration. In the second place, protection was necessary to support capital against the comparative dearness of American labor. As long as a rapid increase of the population and a concomitant decline in the rate of wages was regarded as inevitable and was viewed with complacency, so long this argument carried weight. But with the growth of the popular demand for a higher standard of life it lost its force. Thirdly, the argument that protection would give employment to the unemployed was uttered with tremendous volume during and after the crisis of 1819-20. The argument continued unabated, changing somewhat so as to embrace a policy which would insure the employment of American laborers. Buchanan in 1837, speaking of the laborers in the coal trade, said, "Their rights ought to be protected. To throw them out of employment for the benefit of foreign labor would be both cruel and unjust." The main idea is security of employment and nothing is said concerning competition with the low wages of foreign labor. The speaker had not developed that thought. It was not an essential part of the argument. Finally, the claim that protection would retard migration westward rested necessarily upon the inferences that it would give steady employment and maintain the current rate of wages.

Closely allied to the last two arguments, and naturally developing out of them into a new and more positive doctrine, was the idea that protection was needed against the pauper labor of Europe, to prevent American wages from falling to the level of the latter. This theory received its impetus from the economic, social, and political conditions which prevailed during the period of its early development. Furthermore the reaction toward free-trade, beginning with 1828, created conditions which naturally led to a comparison of American with competing labor. While the tendency had been toward a higher tariff the need for this study had hardly suggested itself, but the removal of certain duties brought in the consideration of the actual effect upon American laborers and stimulated the comparison with European labor. One of the first intimations of the new line of development is found in the remarks of Bates of Massachusetts in Congress in 1828.[1] He gave expression to the following sentiment: "If you hope, therefore, to maintain our system of Government, you must maintain the people at the elevated standard of living, and, as entirely dependent upon it, of moral and intellectual culture which they now hold. This you cannot do if you bring the day laborer, who must earn his $.75 to feed, to clothe, and to school his children, into contact and competition with him who will work for six pence sterling, because he wants and cares for none of these things and because six pence will answer all his purposes."

Between 1828 and 1830 the low wages of seamstresses in Philadelphia attracted considerable attention. Matthew Carey estimated that 12,000 women in Boston, New York, Philadelphia, and Baltimore were ekeing out a precarious existence by the use of the needle and he made strong efforts to ameliorate their condition. He tried to secure a higher rate of wages for them through organization, advocated a greater variety of employments, and even suggested migration to the West. These conditions subsequently became a subject for more discussion in connection with the tariff; so that the relation between tariff and wages began to assume greater importance.

[1] *Cong. Debates,* 4: 2014.

In 1831 in an address before a society of workingmen, the following view was maintained: "We import from other regions where the work is still performed by serfs or slaves and thus bring the hardy yeomanry of our own land, as well as our skillful manufacturers and mechanics, into a ruinous competition with those unfortunate fellow beings of other lands and countries. If one portion of them is oppressed and forced to toil for naught the produce of their labor is employed as a means of depressing the prices of their brethren in other lands. These products are sent here or elsewhere to be offered in competition with similar products of the labor of other men. No wonder then that when all the workingmen of Europe, Asia, and Africa are in a state of comparative slavery, that we of America should find it necessary to interpose the strong arm of Government to protect and cherish our own industries."[2]

That very year a petition to Congress from manufacturers of leather, boots, and shoes stated that a reduction of the duties would aggravate competition with France where wages were low. The petitioners could hardly live now and did not want their wages reduced. The contemporaneous riot at Lowell between Americans and Irishmen called forth the comment that our native workmen would be driven out of manufacturing by the incoming foreigners unless they would work sixteen hours per day and for a few shillings a week. Thus we see that the competition of immigrants was already regarded with some disfavor and the attendant effects were discussed. It required only another step to compare the foreigner engaged in his occupation at home with the American laborer employed in a like trade and to oppose competition upon equal terms.

In 1832 the subject received considerable attention from representatives of Massachusetts and Pennsylvania, states which possessed a large labor population. John Davis declared in Congress that,[3] if protection were abandoned, manufacturing must cease or our wages be reduced to the standard of England

---

[2] Whitcomb, Samuel Jr., *Address before the Workingmen's Society of Dedham*, Sept. 7, 1831.

[3] *Cong. Debates*, 8: 3309.

and Ireland, and our labor be brought into competition with the cheapest labor of those countries; that the policy of the advocates of free-trade was to reduce wages; that he opposed such a policy; and that a lowering of wages would decrease the consumption of the laborer. Other representatives of New England emphasized the importance of labor. Stewart, who resided at Pittsburg—a growing iron center,—was equally emphatic and voiced a similar sentiment. "High-priced and prosperous labor requires protection against low-priced and depressed labor. Our laborer must work for six pence or yield the market to the paupers of England. The reduction of protection would reduce the price of labor in this country."[4] In the State Convention of National Republicans, held at Harrisburg, the effects of foreign competition upon the American laborer and mechanic were vigorously exploited. Reference was made to the reduction of wages to the scantiest pittance, to suspension of labor, and to beggary as following in the wake of a free-trade policy. Pennsylvania was now beginning to consider in earnest the effect of protection and of the reduction of duties upon the laboring classes of the state.

The struggle over the compromise tariff of 1833 added a little to the development and increasing importance of the new doctrine. Webster claimed that the reduction of the duties on shoes, boots, and clothing would bring thousands of mechanics engaged in these industries to ruin, and that the bill in these points aimed a deadly blow against the poor.[5] Dallas of Pennsylvania protested against the unemployment which would be occasioned by the bill. The discussion of the tariff in the Senate, however, hardly touched the labor question, as other critical and overshadowing issues—the question of nullification and the constitutionality of a protective tariff,—were forced to the front in the tariff debates.

In the House of Representatives protection to labor received more attention. The bill proposed a general and gradual reduction of tariff duties and many local industries in the North

[4] *Ibid.*, 3273-4.
[5] *Ibid.*, 9: 728.

and East would be affected. The growth of manufactures and mining had absorbed a large amount of capital, and had increased the number of persons dependent upon these industries. Many complaints were therefore made against the tariff bill. Huntington and Ellsworth of Connecticut argued that the laboring class would suffer. Young declared that our laborers would be depressed to the state of English laborers. Briggs and Choate of Massachusetts claimed that thousands of men would be thrown out of employment and the former maintained that the price of labor would have to be reduced.[6] Bates emphasized his hostility to the competition of American with foreign labor and maintained that lower duties would necessitate working cheaply, living cheaply, and stooping low. Burgess spoke of the competition with the paupers of Europe and the slaves of South Carolina, which free-trade would bring, and insisted that war was being made against the free white labor of the country.[7] John Whipple of Providence, part owner of the Hope cotton mill, testified before a congressional committee that a reduction of duty would stop wages and force the laborers to migrate westward or maintain a scanty subsistence in New England. He added that the direct tendency of the tariff was to keep up the price of labor.[8] The members from Pennsylvania were emphatic in their arguments. McKennan said that protection raised the wages of labor. Denny maintained that the poorer workmen, mechanics, and laborers would suffer, that their wages would be reduced, and that they ought to be protected.

Other protectionists argued along similar lines. The proposed reduction of the tariff had forced them to consider the effect upon the laborers engaged in the industry affected. Formerly they argued that protection would remedy unemployment. Now they claimed that free-trade would aggravate this condition. The argument is similar but the point of observation has changed. In previous controversies they contended that manufactures should be extended in order to insure employment to

[6] *Cong. Debates,* 9: 1043, 1075.
[7] *Ibid.,* 1384
[8] *Ibid.,* 1509

the laboring classes. Manufacturing industry had grown, had absorbed considerable capital formerly engaged in navigation, and had employed thousands of persons. The attack upon the tariff was therefore partly an attack upon established manufactures, and protectionists now defended the interests of the class employed in this industry just as free-traders had formerly maintained the rights of seamen to their employment in commercial pursuits. The greater number of laborers and the increasing favor in which a higher standard of life was held, made it possible to protest against a possible reduction of wages and direct competition with foreign nations. Even then the argument is not entirely comprehensible without a consideration of the facts that the migration of labor to the West was not accomplished without considerable friction; that many laborers were loath to leave their native states and their old home surroundings; and that the eastern states desired to grow and prosper instead of declining to a position of relative inferiority as compared with the West.

The above facts indicate that the pauper labor argument had put in an appearance and had received some attention in 1832 and 1833. The subsequent subsidence of the tariff question prevented the healthy growth of the argument. Although attention had been directed primarily to other subjects, the relatively unimportant discussion of the tariff in 1837 again added to the gathering prestige of this line of reasoning. Davis typifies those giving expression to the doctrine in its advanced form. In the course of the debate he took occasion to utter the following sentiment: "The poor only ask of you that you would pursue toward them an American policy—a policy which will give them good wages for their labor—and they will take care of themselves. They entreat of you not to reduce them to the deplorable condition of the miserable population of foreign countries, by reducing their wages to the same standard. What makes the condition of the laborer so universally prosperous here? How is it that he enjoys the not only great physical but moral comforts and blessings to an extent surpassing that of the laborer in any other country whatever? It is because he is better paid. Break down the business in which it is employed by subjecting it to direct competition with foreign pauperism; lessen the demand for labor by introducing foreign productions, and like causes will produce like results. You will then have as poor and wretched a population as that against which it will in such circumstances contend for bread.''[9]

More conservative and less emphatic is the position of Buchanan who thought that it was both cruel and unjust to throw our workingmen out of employment for the benefit of foreign laborers. Webster, although conservative in his utterances, had also advanced to higher grounds. Our artisans, he said, were the first to be protected by the Constitution. The protection extended under our laws to capital was as nothing to that given to labor. He had now abandoned the idea of protection to capital and had substituted protection to labor. Others did the same. The pauper labor argument—that is, the claim that protection was necessary to maintain the wages of American laborers against the competition of the more poorly paid workingmen of foreign countries—was advanced as a chief cause for continuing the protective policy.

By common consent, the tariff of 1833 was to be left undisturbed until 1842. The agitation for higher duties, however, increased as the latter date approached. Horace Greeley became a strong advocate of protection and exerted a wide influence upon the thought of the hour. He was deeply interested in the welfare of the laboring classes and regarded protection as a measure of great value to them, emphasizing the high wage argument. In 1839,[10] in answer to writers who denied that free-trade reduced wages, he set forth the claim that wages were higher in protection than in free-trade countries. The developing view-points of both the friends and enemies of the tariff were thus distinctly intimated.

As already indicated, the political soil of this period could hardly help but nourish the growth of the high wage argument. Not the tariff only, but other questions as well, felt the influ-

---

[9] *Cong. Debates,* 13: 898.
[10] *Hunt's Magazine,* 1: 417.

ences of the new impulses of the time. Although Harrison hardly touched the tariff question during the campaign of 1840, many northern protectionists realized that a new opportunity to agitate the question had presented itself. Greeley by means of the *Log Cabin*, a temporary campaign newspaper, urged the Whig arguments upon the country and frequently referred to the need of protection. He protested against the depression of the prices of labor, of property, and of produce, and against the stagnation of business. The discrediting of paper money, he said, was partly responsible for these conditions. Likewise the breaking down of the protective policy would expose American labor to an unequal rivalry with that of the oppressed vassals of Europe. Greeley emphasized the need of high wages, and the arguments on different questions were made to converge on this point. Daniel Webster again laid stress upon the importance of a high standard of life. He compared the American with the European laborer and claimed political and economic advantage for the former. He opposed a reduction of American wages and the administration measures which would affect the nominal wages of labor. These themselves had nothing or little to do with the tariff but paved the way for further discussion of the wage argument. Whig celebrations at different places, especially in Pennsylvania, utilized banners inscribed with "No reduction of wages" and "A protective tariff," thus popularizing the new development in the tariff controversy.

In 1842 when the tariff question again became acute, the pauper labor argument received greater attention than ever before. Many protectionists relied upon it as the main argument for a higher tariff. It, in fact, assumed the prominence which it has held ever since. Friends of protection had called a Convention of Home Industry to give impulse to the movement for a higher tariff. Committees were appointed to report on various articles of manufacture, and the subject of labor was also made the basis of one report. Greeley was chairman of this committee. No former convention of this kind had given special attention to the subject of labor. This one, among other things, adopted a resolution demanding protection for labor against the degraded and starving conditions of the laboring classes throughout the world. Greeley's temporary publication, *The American Laborer*, running through a large part of this year, stoutly defended protection and especially asserted its importance to the interests of labor. He utilized the *New York Tribune* for a similar purpose.

The agitation throughout the country was vigorous. Home Leagues held meetings to discuss the tariff.[11] Laborers were invited to come and be convinced that the free admission of goods made by degraded foreigners would not be to their advantage. Facts were presented to show that the hard times affected those industries most which employed the least machinery, and that journeymen, apprentices, and laboring men were most injured. Again it was urged that some foreign countries paid bounties on exported goods and free competition would lower American wages accordingly. Selfish interests likewise took advantage of their opportunities. The iron and paper manufacturers met and discussed the problem of protection.[12] They did not want our labor to work at reduced prices. The boot and shoe dealers at Boston took a similar point of view. Whigs everywhere addressed their appeals to the laborer and defended a high wage. Protectionists[13] in New York wanted a tariff which would protect us from articles competing with the products of American labor, and resolutions to that effect were introduced into the Senate of that state. In New England the argument was extensively used and furnished political capital for friends of the tariff. Even in the West, the need of high wages for the laborer was emphasized. In the North the movement was not confined to the Whigs and many Democrats supported protection to labor.

In the congressional debates on the tariff of 1842 protection to labor was one of the favorite arguments of the high tariff men. Representatives from New England, New York, New Jersey, Pennsylvania, and also from the West demanded protec-

---

[11] *New York Tribune*, January 5, 1842.
[12] *Ibid.*
[13] *Ibid.*, March 26, 1842.

tion on this ground. It was contended that that nation stood highest in moral and physical greatness which gave the highest rate of wages and the largest returns for labor, and that protection to labor meant secure, productive, and steady occupation, free from foreign aggression.

Naturally the strongest appeals on this ground came from the East. Fifty-three of the seventy-two congressional districts in this section, conducting manufacturing and mercantile enterprise, were Whig. The South had fifteen such districts represented by seven Whigs and eight Democrats. The fifty-one farming districts of the East sent but twenty-four Whigs, while the farmers of the West sent an almost solid Whig delegation. (33 to 9). The home market still appealed to the West, but in the East protectionism had its strength largely in the manufacturing districts. Here was the large laboring population. The favorable influences described above, the change in the industrial situation, the temporary depression, and the conditions existing abroad—all cooperated to emphasize the importance of the high wage argument, and to force apparent concessions to the laboring classes.

The Committee on Manufactures in 1842 reported a tariff bill and called attention to the problems involved. This was the first time that such a committee considered the various industries with the view of ascertaining the attendant interests of labor. Special stress was laid upon industries in which labor was the chief element of the product. The importance of the iron and leather manufactures to the laboring classes was pointed out, and the pauper labor of Europe was held responsible, in part, for our industrial depression, while the relatively high American wages were cited as a cause for protection against foreign labor which would otherwise degrade our own.[14] The debate then opened on the floor of Congress where the Democrats had posed as the exclusive friends of the poor and the laboring classes. To these Hudson of Massachusetts made a vigorous reply.[15] He strongly opposed the debasement of American

[14] *27th Cong., 2nd Sess.; Com. Rep., No. 461.*
[15] *Cong. Globe,* **13:** App., 929.

labor, gave statistical evidence indicating the pauper wages of European labor, and urged the need of a tariff which would guarantee fair competition between our own and foreign workingmen. He furthermore maintained that the tariff would raise wages. Other protectionists argued along similar lines. The identity of the interests of the farmers, mechanics, and laborers was proclaimed, while the home market and labor arguments were brought into definite relation and connection with each other. Senator Evans defended the protection principle, contending that a high price for labor was a test of prosperity. The opposition, he argued, favored low prices and low wages, but if a reduction of prices were occasioned, wages would be the first to fall. Choate held that the labor in all our industries ought to be protected, and Huntington of Connecticut declared that protection to labor was necessary for flourishing agriculture and manufacturing. Furthermore the consumer would be benefited. Hardly an advocate of protection failed to refer to the need of protection to labor. The argument itself as presented took three different lines of development; first, the high wages or pauper labor argument which was the most important; second, the claim that a readjustment of the level of prices would be distinctly injurious to the laboring classes; third, protection would increase the demand for labor, hence benefit the laborer by multiplying employment and insuring him a reasonable remuneration. This was the gist of Webster's labor argument in 1840. Greeley in 1843 emphasized this phase, but also referred to the subject of pauper labor.[16]

The law of 1842 was not distinctly a partisan measure, although Whigs and Democrats rallied on opposite sides. In the House 35 Whigs voted against, and 20 Democrats for, the bill. Nineteen of the latter came from New York and Pennsylvania, and nearly all of these represented districts containing a large manufacturing population. The reasons for this vote were later stated as follows, "The argument upon which the tariff of 1842 was sustained was that our manufactures, agriculture, our every

---

[16] Greeley, *Recollections of a Busy Life*, 549.

interest required to be protected against the pauper labor of Europe."[17] Certainly this argument had become an important one in the ammunition of the high tariff party. The revival of the tariff question necessarily filled the country with discussion on the subject. The high wages argument had become the subject of defense and dissection. The Central Committee of Home Leagues in an address set forth the claim that the high standard of the American laborer must be maintained and injurious competition be prevented. Protection newspapers continued to agitate the question, and the direct influence of the new tariff impressed itself upon the public mind. Entirely apart from the merits of protection as a permanent policy, it is undeniable that the tariff of 1842 accelerated the renewal of prosperity.[18] Iron, cotton, and woolen mills revived and many wage earners again found employment. A period of general business activity followed.

The different influences before mentioned continued to make possible the growth of the high wage argument and some of our manufacturers employed their efforts to enhance its apparent importance. In 1844 therefore, the Whig party, assembled in convention, dared to express itself in favor of a "tariff for revenue to defray the necessary expenses of the Government and discriminating with special reference to the protection of the domestic labor of the country."[19] Other arguments were subordinated, and the new one was hereafter to be of paramount importance. The discussion of the tariff in and out of Congress that year added nothing to the growth of protection theory, hence it is necessary to turn to 1846 when the subject again received consideration in detail.

The Democratic party being again in power sought to revise the tariff. The southern wing was in control and the former Democratic protectionists of the North were forced to become lukewarm toward this doctrine. A comparatively easy victory

[17] *Cong. Globe,* **13:** App., 495. Speech of Wright, of New York.
[18] See discussion of effect of this act in Taussig, *Tariff History of the U. S.,* 119–21. Also Bishop, *History of Manufactures,* **2:** 448.
[19] *New York Tribune,* May 11, 1844.

by the opponents of the Act of 1842 was the result. The supporters of protection, however, stoutly defended their principle, placed added emphasis upon protection to American labor, and gave to that doctrine a completeness which required but little subsequent refinement. Severance of Maine,[20] alluded to the volume of our laboring population, to their consuming power, to the need of creating a demand for labor, to the migration westward which would result from free trade, and to the opposition to the abolition of slavery because it would enhance the price of labor, also to the fact that hard times caused disproportionate suffering among the poorer people. Davis of Massachusetts,[21] in advancing the pauper labor argument, contended that not only economic loss but a diminution of moral and mental culture was the necessary consequence of a low tariff policy. Stewart emphasized the same consideration as did the last named speaker, but also called attention to the political insignificance to which the poorly paid laborer will decline. Winthrop, however, struck even more closely the characteristic point of the high wage argument in the following words: "Protection looks at the workingman not in his mere brute capacity, as a consumer, but in his higher nature as a producer. It looks not to reducing the price of what he eats or what he wears, but to keeping up the price of his own labor. It looks, in short, to wages first, wages last, wages altogether."[22]

Thus we have in the arguments of these men the complete emergence of the doctrine that protection preserves the high wages of the American workmen against the competition of the pauper labor of Europe. It took the form of protection against the product of labor, not against the labor itself. Either method was said to amount to the same result, but immigration was not then considered an important problem and restriction was said to be contrary to our traditional policy. Strong friends of labor as well as capitalists maintained this principle. It is true that

[20] *Cong. Globe*, **16:** App , 705.
[21] *Ibid.*, 1114.
[22] *Ibid.*, 973.

in subsequent discussion[23] the proper amount of protection was computed to be the difference between the labor cost of producing a good here and the similar cost abroad, but the essential characteristics of the argument had now been imparted to it. The manner in which it was met by the opposition, in turn, assists in explaining the cause of its rise and throws light upon various movements of the time. We shall, therefore, briefly point out the attitude of the free-trade party.

In a previous chapter we have shown that the ablest free-traders, such as Gallatin, had pointed out the relation between labor and wages when that subject was first discussed, and had suggested the chief cause of high wages; viz., the abundance of cheap lands, the productivity of labor, and the insufficient supply of laborers. In the earlier decades when the general attitude toward wages was a negative one, the burden of the problem rested heavily upon the protectionists. Free-traders merely pointed to the difference between wages here and abroad, and discussed the theoretical considerations which determined the difference. With the growth of ameliorative tendencies and the assumption of a positive program in respect to wages by protectionists, free-traders were forced to analyze the bearing of their theories upon the actual conditions of the time. They faced a concrete situation in a progressive nation where added economic advantage did not cover the entire gamut of the workingman's interests. The new problem for the opponents of the tariff was the relation of free-trade to the general elevation of an ambitious and independent laboring class. Unfortunately the abstract economist who thinks internationally often supplies with arguments unchanged the politician and legislator who think nationally or more often sectionally, and these arguments the latter attempt to apply to conditions illy fitted to become the subject of extensive theorizing. The sectional aspect of the tariff con-

---

[23] The following is a specimen of the argument which became current: "When foreign labor which costs one—or its products which are the same thing—comes into the same market on a free trade platform with American labor which costs three—or with its products which are the same thing—it is absurd to suppose that American labor will still maintain the relative value of three to one. They must both come to the same level." Colton, *Public Economy*, 65.

fused the defense of the free-traders and hindered the development of the refutation of the high wages argument.

The existence of slavery in the South and the championship of that system influenced southern free-traders in their attitude toward labor. Low wages in the South were viewed with comparative complacency. The dignity and worth of labor was yet but dimly realized there. Accordingly a defense of high wages was difficult, and the artificial stimulation of the price of labor was severely criticised. Even in 1842 the minority of the committee on manufactures declared that if manufacturers would not reduce wages they should be forced to decrease their profits, that the consumer would not pay the cost of a high wage when a low wage only was demanded in the South for a similar service.[24] Free-traders, however, began to develop several lines of attack. Calhoun[25] in 1840 vigorously assailed the protectionists' position, contending that high wages were due to the effectiveness of industry, and that only those high wages caused in this way were an evidence of prosperity. Two years later he declared that wages were but the residuum after deducting the profit of capital and the expense of production including the exaction of the Government in the shape of taxes; that as the latter decreased, wages would increase, and that prices might fall and wages rise at the same time—a combination most favorable to the laborer. Here Calhoun recognized the laborer both as a producer and a consumer; both lines of argument were used by the opponents of the tariff.

That a protective tariff, under the conditions which obtained during the period of tariff controversy, would maintain the wages of many American workingmen could hardly be doubted. Even so ardent a statesman as McDuffie admitted that it raised the wages of manufacturing labor. It was necessary, therefore, to analyze the laboring population and to point out how few were directly dependent upon the tariff. Protectionists had insisted that the entire laboring population was benefited thereby.

---

[24] *27th Cong., 2nd Sess., Rep., No. 461.*
[25] Speech in the U. S. Senate, February 5, 1840.

Smith of Virginia,[26] replying to this argument in 1842, computed that only 265,000 laborers were employed in factories directly, that nearly that number of mechanics were dependent upon agriculture, and that less than one-third of the laborers would be affected by the tariff directly. Another speaker[27] contended that out of the 791,000 workmen in manufacturing and mechanical pursuits, according to the census of 1840, an analysis showed that only 284,351 were engaged in protected industries. Various estimates were made tending to show that only a small per cent. of the American people could be benefited and this at the expense of the remainder. We were exporting goods and competing abroad with foreign labor—a fact which free-traders employed to show the possibility of a like competition if the goods were brought to our shores. Our improvement in efficiency, it was argued, was sufficient to cover the difference in the cost of labor, but even if the contrary were true, protection was not yet justified.[28] Furthermore the difference between wages here and in England was slight—a statement quite true of the wages of certain skilled laborers, but one not generally reliable. The additional contention that the contest was not between high and low wages but between human labor and machinery received some consideration, in view of the fact that the increased use of the latter had caused temporary displacements of labor. On the whole, the efficiency of American labor was properly emphasized, but this fact, coupled with the frequent admission that labor in the North was benefited by protection, rendered the defense inadequate. The argument in reference to the laborer as a producer and to his nominal wage under the two systems needed the support of the claims concerning the effect of protection upon the real wages of the laborer, upon his double capacity as a producer and a consumer.

Gallatin, when the wage argument first made its appearance, vigorously emphasized the importance of the real wages of the laborer. While the earlier tariff discussions concerned them-

---

[26] *Cong. Globe,* **13:** App., 726.
[27] Burke, Hon. Edmund, *The Protective System.* Washington, 1846.
[28] *Cong. Globe,* **13:** App., 114, 484.

selves with the consumer, the laboring classes, owing to their unimportance, failed to receive much attention as such. The hardships incurred owing to duties on the necessaries of life were urged against the protective policy. The opposition to the duties on coal, salt, etc., after the Compromise of 1833 had the consumer's interests in mind. During the controversy between 1840 and 1846, however, the laborer as a consumer received ample consideration. In this connection the free-trader more emphatically assumed the offensive, pointing out that a tariff on goods would lessen the real wages of labor, and the laborer would receive no share of the benefits of the tariff. In many cases, indeed, the competition between laborers prevented them from securing an advance in nominal wages. The diminution in the wages of many cotton mill employees after 1842, and the reply of various manufacturers that they were suffering from domestic, not foreign, competition, served to accentuate the insistence of the free-traders upon the importance of the real wage. Boot and shoe makers of New York City held a meeting in 1845 and opposed the tariff of 1842, claiming that it increased the price of stock which they manufactured and also of nearly all the articles which they consumed, and that it was a cause of the depression in their business. Secretary Walker,[29] in his report of 1845, declared that wages had not advanced after the tariff of 1842, but his statement is necessarily erroneous in view of the subsequent revival of business. He more truthfully asserted, however, that the tariff fell more heavily upon the poor. Many laboring men opposed protection for the same reason, claiming that their wages were not affected, but that their cost of living was. The reaction against the tariff of 1842, culminating in the Act of 1846, was to a considerable extent brought about by a spread of opinions of this nature.

A defect of increasing importance in the wage argument was its attitude toward the immigrant. As before indicated, Seth Luther had in the early thirties pointed out the inconsistency of protectionists in admitting workmen freely from abroad, but

---

[29] Taussig, *State Papers on the Tariff*, 226.

objecting to the free importation of goods. So in 1842 it was maintained that if protection was necessary, the cheap labor planting itself among us needed to be feared. A few years later, Wilmot of Pennsylvania, in examining the motives of the manufacturers, quite correctly charged them with expressing no alarm over the immigration of cheap labor, and he furthermore claimed that they were actually attempting to depress the price of labor. Nor were protectionists dismayed over the importation of labor-saving machinery. John Pickering[30] in 1847 stated the case in the following vigorous words: "Therefore if the working classes will promote the 'protective system,' their first object should be to prevent the importation of foreign 'pauper operatives;' it will then be time enough to think about preventing the importation of the goods they make; till then it would be perfectly useless." In this manner one of the great weaknesses of the wage argument was continually punctured and exposed to public ridicule. Many workingmen in the East were beginning to feel the competition of the immigrant and they opposed a system which seemed to provide a sham defense only.

The position of the western lands in maintaining and advancing the current rate of wages has already been explained. Many southern men who believed that their section was taxed for the benefit of northern capital and perhaps of northern labor also, became more earnest in their support of the favorite western proposition to reduce the price of the public lands. Secretary Walker[31] in his well-known report voiced the sentiments of the

---

[30] *The Working Man's Political Economy*, 150.

[31] "But while the tariff does not enhance the wages of labor, the sales of the public lands at low prices......would accomplish this object......The power of the manufacturing capitalist in reducing the wages of labor would be greatly diminished. Reduce the price which the laborer must pay for the public domain;......prevent all speculation and monopoly in the public lands; confine the sales to settlers and cultivators in limited quantities;......reduce the taxes by reducing the tariff and bringing down the prices which the poor are thus compelled to pay for all the necessaries of life, and more will be done for the benefit of American labor than if millions were added to the profits of manufacturing capital by the enactment of a protective tariff." On the other hand, Walker's position in respect to the relation of labor and capital was expressed as follows: "When the number of manufactures is not great the power of the system to regulate the wages of labor is inconsiderable; but as the profit of capital, invested in manufactures, is augmented by the protective tariff, there is a corresponding in-

free-traders who believed this measure to be a more effectual means of preserving the high wages of labor and that without great cost to the remainder of our people. By reducing the price of lands to nominal figures and confining the sale to actual settlers, laborers could hardly be deprived of the alternative of becoming independent if good wages were not paid by manufacturers. Protection had been the stimulus the East demanded to accelerate her growth and retain her working population. Free land was Walker's remedy for diminishing wages but it implied the migration of the laborer to the West.

---

crease of power until the control of such capital over the wages of labor becomes irresistible. As this power is exercised from time to time, we find it resisted by combinations among the working classes......But the government, by protective duties, arrays itself on the side of the manufacturing system, and by thus augmenting its wealth and power soon terminates in its favor the struggle between man and money—between capital and labor."

CHAPTER VII

CONCLUSION

In the foregoing pages we have attempted to review briefly the causes and development of the labor argument for protection. We have seen that the extraordinary conditions ending with peace with England in 1815, and especially the few years of war with that country had given manufacturing enterprise a decided impetus. A large amount of capital had been invested in various industries, and many women and children had been employed. A considerable amount of labor primarily engaged in other industries had also assisted the growth of manufactures. The demand in 1816 for protection was accordingly supported by several arguments. It was claimed that industries established during the war should not be allowed to perish; that a parallel development of all our industries was necessary; that a home market was needed; that we should become independent of foreign nations; furthermore that labor formerly of no value was now made useful and that this labor should be continued in employment. Hamilton had stated the labor argument long before. Now when the time was ripe it was reiterated and given a new emphasis. The argument itself was not that of a "restrictionist." Protectionists usually disclaimed any intention of foisting such a system upon the country. On the other hand an ambitious and youthful nation would be likely to look with favor upon a policy which would employ all its available labor. Thus the form of the labor argument used in 1816 in connection with the appeal to support the cotton industry came into vogue and continued to be urged as long as the industrial and labor conditions and the ideals of the times allowed.

It cannot be over-emphasized that the more fruitful discussion of the tariff has been in relation to its practical operation and that theoretical considerations have had less weight. The latter are the arguments used by the body opposing the policy. Nor has the economic motive been the only actuating one. Furthermore the freely expressed attitude toward the laborer naturally gave to both protectionists and free-traders their characteristic arguments. The former pointed to the better paid workmen abroad and claimed our laborers were securing but little more, hence a protective policy would be justified. The latter emphasized the differences and concluded that such a policy would be injurious. This was largely done, not after consultation with the laboring man, but quite apart from his wishes. The lack of interest in the elevation of the working classes was only too evident. The years 1819–20, however, inaugurated a change and the mechanic appears as a factor in tariff controversy and usually as an adherent of the protective principle. The subject of unemployment had suddenly become an important one. The need of work for the laborer was boldly exploited, and the argument when used at critical times has usually been effective. The earlier point of view was concerned with security of employment, and not with a desire to raise wages. High wages were in fact considered as one of the disadvantages with which American manufactures were forced to cope. Still the importance of steady employment, quite apart from the rate of wages, was realized; the opposing parties differing of course as to the method of securing this desideratum.

The rise of the laboring classes, numerically, politically, economically; the advent of better ideals; the enlarging contact with foreign labor, owing to increased immigration; and the sectional aspect which the tariff began to assume, forced attention to the subject of wages. Not only the master mechanic but the journeyman and the ordinary laborer in the factories and on the farms, became important. The girls in the cotton mills were indeed among the first to demand higher standards. A transformation of the labor argument became necessary. The divergence, however, from the older position is not an abrupt one but clearly expresses the dawning of a new era. Webster is a link joining the old to the new. Security of employment with less emphasis upon its effect upon wages was the burden of his argument. Preservation of the American wage against the competition of poorly paid foreign labor was demanded by Stewart, John Davis, and later by Kelley and others. Foreign labor conditions now served a different purpose. The improvement in America had proceeded more rapidly than abroad, consequently protectionists found it advantageous to indicate the great difference between wages here and abroad, instead of minimizing them as formerly. The change was less a new attitude toward the facts than a change in the attitude toward labor. The high wage argument must be explained largely in connection with this important fact. This is the more apparent when one realizes its similarity to that of the wages argument made against the Independent Treasury bill about the same time. Nor did the free-traders immediately abandon their former position. Their policy was a cautious one. In common with their opponents many of them still cited the low wages of English workmen, but often with a different purpose than formerly. Then it was to indicate the absurdity of protection; now to show the injurious and pernicious economic effect of protection upon the workingmen, the moral and political effects having from the beginning received considerable emphasis. It is but slowly that advocates of free-trade crystallize their opposition to the high wage argument by emphasizing the chief causes of high wages and calling attention to the consumers' interests. The liberation of the American mind from sectional bias would have simplified the labor argument, but this could not be realized.

Sectionalism as a factor in evolving the wage argument can not be overlooked. Both South and West were agricultural. The latter was formerly a unit for protection, but by 1842 many of its leaders had joined the South against the protective policy, which restricted migration to the new lands and in part sustained the efforts of the East to retain its growth. The high wages argument for protection was largely an eastern argument. True, the contrast between free and slave labor accomplished another line of territorial cleavage, but the leading spirits of the argument were eastern men. Clay and western men in Congress did, indeed, advocate protection to American labor, but usually in connection with its reputed advantage to the agricultural interests. The occasional western presentation of the high wages argument, however, neglected this and simply bore evidence of the importance of eastern influence or of the psychology of partisan politics. The various movements which culminated in the demand for higher wages were not all distinctively eastern, yet the laboring classes were largely confined to that section, so the cry for protection against foreign labor would naturally be more urgent there than elsewhere. The somewhat tardy recognition by the South of the need of higher wages added to the importance attached to the argument. The South could hardly be expected to have agreed with the East on this point. The interests of the two sections differed, and the possibility of paying high wages was necessary to insure the future progress of the East. The relation of each section to the tariff and to the high wages argument becomes clearer when the conditions of progress are thus indicated.

The theory of wages held by American controversialists necessarily affected the growth of the argument. Although the immediate and practical bearings of protection were the most important points at issue, the theoretical background can not be omitted. The local influence of the unsettled western lands in buoying up the standard rate of wages was generally admitted. The connection between wages and the productivity of labor was less clearly understood and this misapprehension was the cause of much fallacy in argument. Francis A. Walker,[1] however, in asserting that the "speeches of Clay, Stewart, and Kelley have significance only on the assumption that one day's work here is worth one day's work elsewhere" neglected entirely the sectional aspect of the controversy—certainly a very prom-

[1] *Wages*, 41.

inent feature. Yet his point is a strong one, for the importance of productivity was inadequately treated, especially by protectionists. Henry Carey[2] did point out that productivity influenced the wages of the laborer. Gallatin,[2] on the other hand, spoke of skill and productivity, but urged the all-inclusiveness of the indefinite demand-and-supply of labor. Calhoun[2] in his contention that wages depended upon the effectiveness of labor spoke more to the point, and the development of this idea placed the free-trade contention on firmer ground. With the growth of free-trade sentiment in the North and West, this factor received new development; real wages were emphasized; and free-traders began to explain away the difference between American and English wages on natural grounds, and to belittle the reputed high wages of domestic labor. Formerly they had pointed to the great gap which existed between the two. On the other hand, an indetermination to work out the effects of competition in the long run, and stress upon the immediate result upon the class of labor affected, marked the attitude of the protectionist.

The protective system has been an historic product, its growth and decline depending upon political and economic circumstances. As is well known, protection was at first regarded as a temporary policy, and only subsequently did its advocates demand its indefinite continuation. Certain arguments, likewise, partly valid when first promulgated, are no longer applicable, but the force of inertia has carried them on and they are still used with effect. The high wage argument was not only an historic outgrowth but represents in part an ingenious opportunism. A logical development of the argument would require protection against the immigration of the so-called pauper labor itself. Curiously enough the application of the doctrine has been a one-sided one. The exclusion of the Chinese and of alien contract labor marks the limit of its progress along these lines. American labor has never stood unitedly for this doctrine, although that of certain industries has been quite unanimous in its favor. At the time of its inception many laborers denied

---

[2] See references cited.

the validity of the argument. Others directly affected by foreign competition asked for protection. Many were not concerned with the question. It is hardly possible to determine the direct influence exerted by labor itself upon the growth of the high wage argument. It was the indirect influence effected by the upward pressure of the class, which more largely represents the contribution of labor to this new line of development. The labor vote, however, has been an important item. The Whig platform of 1844 betrays this fact as do other platforms of later date. The capture of Pennsylvania by the Republicans is said to have been consummated by a similar line of action. Other states have been held to protection in the same way, but certain classes of labor only have been instrumental agents in its behalf.

The argument has received but little academic support, the majority of economists having denied its validity, but it is generally recognized that in a progressive society a protective tariff may temporarily maintain the nominal wages of a particular class of workmen; that is, if the industry affected depends upon the tariff for its existence. Here, however, the tariff is considered neither nationally nor yet sectionally, but only in relation to a single industry—an inadequate basis for the continuation of a tariff system. Besides this, the advantage claimed is for nominal, rather than for real, wages.

When the wage argument was first urged a large percentage of the laboring class was found in more or less protected industries. Even the opponents of the tariff of 1842 generally admitted that practically one third of the 791,000 laborers would be benefited by protection although at the expense of the rest of the American people, and especially of the agricultural portion. At present the number of laborers affected directly by the tariff is exceedingly small. Bullock has estimated it at from 5 per cent. to 10 per cent. of the total laboring population.[3] Edward Atkinson computed the number directly concerned as approximately 600,000—about 2 per cent. of the entire number

---

[3] *Introduction to the Study of Economics,* 373 (Revised Ed.).

engaged in gainful occupations.[4] The slightness of the apparent advantage to labor at once become manifest. Even though artificial wages at the expense of the consumer were justifiable, one can hardly conclude otherwise than that the once comparatively useful doctrine that protection maintains American wages is little more than an anachronism. Like many other institutions that have outlived their usefulness it has an unusual tenacity of life, and has projected itself from the past into the present, because it has not met adequate resistance. Protection as an offset to the influence of the free lands of the West is explicable, but free lands no longer regulate wages. Yet the sectional aspect of the tariff has been nationalized. Alternative employment for the laborer is, however, quite unavailable. Besides, increased immigration diminishes whatever prospects may open along such lines. The rapid occupancy of the West after the Civil War transformed thousands of possible laborers into farmers, and the development of transportation accelerated this movement. The hardships incurred in the semi-arid districts during the decade 1880–1890 and their subsequent depopulation indicated that the limit of cultivable free lands had been reached, at least until new methods of agriculture were employed. The strength of the impulse to settle upon the accessible lands that remained is seen in the frantic rush to Oklahoma, Indian Territory, and other reservations at their opening. The wages and the condition of the western farmer were preferred to conditions elsewhere. It is evident that protection to labor as a sectional policy had an animus not contained in the present day concept of protection to American labor. Conditions have changed fundamentally since the advent of this doctrine. The historic conditions surrounding its growth render its development comprehensible. The sectional interests involved gave it a natural impetus, while self-seeking manufacturers also encouraged the doctrine. Other causes for its growth have already been mentioned.

No student of tariff history can afford to forget that our

---

[4] *Facts and Figures,* 42.

tariff policy has been an historical development, that it must be interpreted in connection with the contemporaneous facts of history, and that the high wages doctrine deserves the same liberal treatment. In the preceding pages, accordingly, we have endeavored to trace the growth of the labor argument for protection and to show how it culminated in the so-called "pauper labor" or high wages, argument; which, however, under conditions totally different from those obtaining at the time of its inception, can be regarded in no other light than as a "survival."

BIBLIOGRAPHY

Tariff and Manufactures

Batchelder, Samuel, Introduction and Early Progress of the Cotton Manufactures in the United States.
Bishop, J. L., History of Manufactures. 2 Vols.
Bolles, A. S., Financial History of the United States.
Carey, H. C., Harmony of Interests.
—— Past, Present and Future.
Carey, Matthew, Clippings (Ridgeway Library, Philadelphia).
—— Crisis.
—— Essays on Political Economy.
—— Miscellaneous Essays.
—— Olive Branch.
Colton, Calvin, Public Economy.
Coxe, T., Address to Friends of American Manufactures. Aug. 9, 1787.
Denslow, Van Buren, Principles of the Economic Philosophy of Society, Government and Industry.
Depew, C., A Hundred Years of American Commerce.
Dew, T. R., Lectures on the Restrictive System. Richmond, 1829.
Dewey, D. R., Financial History of the United States.
Elliot, O. L., The Tariff Controversy.
Harris, C. W., The Sectional Struggle.
Houston, D. F., A Study of Nullification in South Carolina.
Industrial Commission, Final Report of. (XIX.)
Lewis, E. C., History of the American Tariff.
Low, A. M., Protection in the United States.
Mason, D. H., Short Tariff History of the United States.
Patten, S. N., Economic Basis of Protection.

Powell, E. P., Nullification and Secession in the United States.
Rabbeno, Ugo., American Commercial Policy.
Raguet, Condy., Principles of Free Trade.
Stanwood, E., American Tariff Controversies of the Nineteenth Century. 2 Vols.
Sumner, W. G., Lectures on the History of Protection in the United States.
Taussig, F. W., Tariff History of the United States.
—— State Papers and Speeches on the Tariff.
Thompson, R. E., Protection to Home Industry.
United States Documents, American State Papers. Finance. 8 Vols.
    Among the most important documents are
        Finance II. Digest of Manufactures.
        Finance III. Protection to the Manufacturers of Cotton Fabrics.
—— Annals of Congress.
—— Census Reports. 1820, 1830, 1840.
—— Compilation of the Messages and Papers of the Presidents.
—— Congressional Debates.
—— Congressional Globe.
—— Digest of Accounts of Manufacturing Establishments. Washington, 1823.
—— Pauper Immigration. 25th Cong., 2d Sess., Reports of Committees, **5**: No. 1040.
—— Reports on Finance. 1815–1823.
—— Report of Sec. Walker. 29th Cong., 1st Sess., Exec. Doc., **2**: No. 6.
—— Report on Tariff Bill. 27th Cong., 2d Sess., Reports of Committees, **2**: No. 461.
——Statistical View of the Population of the United States, 1790–1830.
Young, J. P., Protection and Progress.

LABOR

Aiken, John, Labor and Wages at Home and Abroad. 1849.
Bolen. Geo., Getting a Living.

Busey, S. C., Immigration, Its Evils and Consequences.
Carey, H. C., The Rate of Wages.
Ely, R. T., The Labor Movement in America.
Levasseur, P. E., The American Workman.
Luther, Seth., Address to Workingmen of New England.
McMaster, J. B., Acquisition of Political, Social and Industrial Rights of Man in America.
McNeill, Geo. E., The Labor Movement.
Pickering, John, The Working Man's Political Economy.
Powderly, T. V., Thirty Years of Labor.
Report of the Massachusetts Bureau of Statistics of Labor, 1885.
Robinson, Harriet H., Loom and Spindle.
Schoenhof, J., The Economy of High Wages.
Scoresby, William, American Factories and their Female Employees.
Simpson, Stephen, Working Man's Manual.
Simons, J. C., Class Struggle in America.
Walker, F. A., Wages.
Wright, Carroll D., The Industrial Evolution of the United States.
Whitcomb, Samuel, Jr., Address before the Workingmen's Society of Dedham.

Newspapers, Magazines, and Pamphlets

Address of Friends of Domestic Industry, 1831.
American Laborer, 1842.
American Sentinel, 1830.
American System, The. Nathan Hale's Press, 1828.
Blackwood's Magazine, 1825.
Cincinnati Republican, 1828.
Convention of Home Industry, 1841.
Free Trade Pamphlets. (Wisconsin Historical Society.)
Hunt's Magazine.
Log Cabin, 1840.
Mechanic's Free Press, 1828–1831.
Mechanic's Magazine, **1, 2, 3, 4.** Boston.

Memorial of Free Trade Convention, 1831. (Philadelphia.)
New World.
New York American, 1819–1836.
New York Tribune, 1842–1846.
New Yorker.
National Gazette, 1828.
National Intelligencer, 1819.
Niles' Register.
Philadelphia Advertiser, 1819.
Philadelphia Public Ledger, 1836.
Philadelphia Society for Promotion of Domestic Industry.
Plain Sense on National Industry. G. L. Birch and Co., N. Y. 1820.
Protection Pamphlets. (Wisconsin Historical Society.)
Raguet, Condy, Banner of the Constitution.
—— Examiner.
—— Free Trade Advocate.
Western Spy. Cincinnati, 1818.

Miscellaneous Works

Atkinson, Edward, Facts and Figures.
Bancroft, H. H., History of Utah.
Benton, T. H., Abridgement of Debates of Congress.
—— Thirty Years' View.
Bromwell, W. J., History of Immigration to the United States, 1856.
Bullock, Charles J., Introduction to the Study of Economics.
Calhoun, J. C., Works.
Casson, H. N., Organized Self Help.
Darby Tour.
Dickens, Charles, Notes on America.
Fearon's Sketch of the United States.
Flint, James, Early Western Travels. (Thwaites' Ed.)
Gibbins, H. de B., Economic and Industrial Progress of the Century.
Greeley, Horace, Political Economy.

—— Recollections of a Busy Life.
Hall, James, Statistics of the West. Cincinnati, 1836.
Hammond, M. B., The Cotton Industry.
Holmes, J., Account of the United States.
Lossing, B. J., Empire State.
MacGregor, John., Progress of America. London, 1847.
McMaster, J. B., History of the People of the United States, 5.
Meyers, G., History of Tammany Hall.
Newman, S. P., Elements of Political Economy.
Parton, James, Life of Jackson.
Potter, A., Political Economy.
Scharf, J. T., and Westcott, T., History of Philadelphia.
Sharpless, I., History of Pennsylvania.
Smith, W. H., A Political History of Slavery.
Smith, Goldwin, History of the United States.
Tucker, George, Progress of the United States.
Webster, Daniel, Works.

INDEX

Agriculture, importance of, 9; Tench Coxe on, 13; laborers of the East attracted by, 25.
American System, defense of, 71.
Baldwin, Henry remarks on crisis, 34.
Barbour, J. S., on meaning of high wages, 53; on servility of factory laborers, 48.
Bates, I. C., higher standards of life favored by, 85; argument of, on pauper labor. 88.
Bell, John, views of, on tariff, 65.
Benton, Thomas, favors protection, 56; becomes opponent of high tariff, 61.
Bishop. J. L., on unemployment, 31.
Buchanan, James, position of, on tariff, 72.
Calhoun, J. C., on national development, 14; on cause of high wages, 98.
Carey. Henry, on wages of mechanics, 39; on dearness of American labor, 40.
Carey, Matthew, position on public questions, 31; describes depression, 32; advocates protection, 32: argument of, against free-trade, 50; on low wages of seamstresses, 85.
Channing, W. E., on pauper labor, 79.
Children, employment of, 22; child labor favored, 23; wages of, 38; number in textile industries, 76.
Clay, Henry, spokesman for West, 34; denies existence of high wages, 55.
Commerce, early development of, 10.
Convention of "Friends of American Industry," oppose extensive Westward migration, 60.
Cooper, Thomas, views on high tariff, 54.
Cotton, extent of industry, 11; exports of, 11: legislation on, in tariff of 1816. 24; attacked, 63; low price of, 65.

Coxe, Tench, on agriculture, 13; on employment of women, 22.
Davis, John, urges pauper labor argument, 87, 89.
Democratic Party, attracts labor vote, 81; divided on law of 1842, 94; favors low tariff, 95.
Denslow, V., on unemployment, 31.
Denny, Harmar, interests of labor defended by, 88.
East, the, slow growth of, 25, 60; divided, on tariff, 51; favors protection. 61, 106; dispersion of population opposed by, 61; labor problem in, 65.
England, employment of women in, 23; machinery in, 27; condition of labor in, 54.
Everett, Edward, attitude on labor problem, 69.
Export Trade, importance of, 11.
Factory system, development of, 18; struggle against, ceases, 49.
Foote resolution, sectional aspect of, 59.
Free trade, arguments for, 48, 57; defense of, by Gallatin, 64.
Free-trade Convention, admits exceptions to bad influence of restrictive system, 62, 63; contends that real wages are decreased by protection, 67.
Gallatin, Albert, gives account of industry, 21; analyzes wages, 64, 107.
Greeley, Horace, idealism of, 79; favors protection to labor, 90; publisher of the "American Laborer," 92.
Hamilton, Alex., report of, on manufactures, 15; nature of labor argument used, 16.
Harrison, W. H., called "Poor man's friend." 82.
Hayne. R. Y., claims protection favors North only, 66.

INDEX.

Home market argument, importance of in West, 17; support of, by Clay, 55.
Humanitarianism, growth of, 79.
Immigration, early attitude toward, 42; desired by Rush, 42; suffers from crisis of, 1819. 43; retarded by English laws, 43; increase of, 65; opposed, 75; investigation of problem of, 80; relation of, to protection, 101.
Imports, of British goods protested against, 57.
Industrial depression, of 1819-20, 29; of 1837, 77.
Jackson, Andrew, supported by laboring classes, 81.
Jefferson, Thomas, physiocratic opinions of, 10.
Lowell, visited by Jackson, 63; riot in, 86.
Luther, Seth, protection denounced by, 67; on child labor, 76.
Labor, problems of, concerned with tariff question, 20; high wages of, 35; wages of agricultural labor, 37; conditions of, in England, 54; real price of, discussed, 67; lack of sympathy for, 73; Boston Convention of, 75; New York Convention of, 76; appeal to by protectionists, 89.
Laboring classes, organizations among, 74; publications upholding interests of, 74; influence of immigration on, 80; influence on tariff argument, of development of, 104.
Machinery, in England, 27; in woolen industry, 27; in America, 28; patents on, 68.
Madison, James, defends policy of attracting immigrants, 62.
Manufactures, character of goods made, 12; attitude toward, 14; Hamilton's report on, 15; amount of, 18; number employed in, 19, 31, 78, 108; dependence promoted by, 48; moral objections to, 49; leading states in, 78.
McDuffie, Geo., opposes protection, 52; on price of labor, 66; influence of protection on wages admitted by, 98.
Mechanics. the importance of, 26; classes of, 26; defense of, 34; wages of, 39.
National Republicans, interests of labor defended by, 87.

Niles' Register, on value of protection to labor, 70.
Pauper Labor Argument, employment of, by Whitcomb, 86; by laborers, 86; by Davis, 87; by Stewart, 87; first appearance of, 89; importance of, in 1842, 91; form of, 96; application of, to Chinese, 107; present significance of, 109.
Pennsylvania, attitude of, on tariff, 32; injury to, from crisis of 1837, 79; protection to labor favored by, 88; capture of, by Republicans, 108.
Pickering, John. inconsistency of protective sytem denounced by, 101.
Poverty, amount of, in 1819, 30; in 1837, 77.
Protection, constitutionality of, discussed, 33; defense of, by Matthew Carey, 50; early arguments for, 57; supporters of, study English conditions, 70; argument for, 1828-37, 72; defense of, by home-leagues, 92; number of laborers benefited by, 99, 108; development of—an historic product—107; little academic support of, 108.
Raguet, Condy, occasional idleness admitted by, 64; on wages in textile industries, 68.
Rankin, C., interests of commerce defended by, 53.
Rush, Benj., immigration favored by, 42; morals of manufacturing classes defended by, 49; diffusion of population opposed by, 60; dearness of labor denied by, 68.
Sectionalism, Foote resolution dependent on, 59; influence of, 105.
South, foreign trade of, 12; free-trade favored by, 51; attitude of, on protection influenced by low price of cotton, 65; attitude of, toward wages, 98.
States Rights Doctrine, protection hindered by, 47.
Stewart, A., pauper labor argument advanced by, 87.
Tammany, protection favored by, 33.
Tariff legislation, phase of labor argument used in 1816, 48; of 1824, support of, by West, 55; of 1842, support of, not distinctly partisan, 94; renewal of prosperity after, 95; of 1846, enactment of, by Democrats, 96.

INDEX.

Trades Unions, low wages opposed by, 76.
Unemployment, former unimportance of, 28; influence of, on tariff legislation, 28; amount of, in 1819. 31.
Van Buren, M., distrust of, by labor, 82.
Wages, fall of, after War of 1812, 30; cause of high wages, 35; low wages in England, 36; of agricultural labor, 36, 37; of factory employees, 38, 39; of women and children, 38; attitude of organizations toward, 76; low wages of seamstresses, 85; theories of, 106.
Walker, Robert, denied that tariff had increased wages, 100; position of, on land question, 102.
Webster, Daniel, existence of idleness denied by, 34; free-trade supported by, 52; protection to labor favored by, 71; reduction of duties opposed by, 87.

West, the, rapid growth of, 26, 60; home market desired by, 34; protection favored by, 51.
Whig Party, interest in labor developed by, 81; high wages defended by, 92; strength of, in Congress, 93; protection to labor favored by, 94.
Whitcomb, Samuel, protection against pauper labor favored by, 86.
Wilmot, David, on motives of manufacturers, 101.
Women, importance of, in industry, 21; 23; displacement of native women by foreign, 24; wages of, 38; strike among, 74.
Wool and Woolens. legislation on, 63; manufacturers of, discontented, 68.
Workingmen's Party, formation of, 80; platform of, 81; influence of, 82.
Young, Ebenezer, comparison of wages here and abroad, by, 68; pauper labor argument urged by, 88.

American Labor: From Conspiracy to Collective Bargaining

AN ARNO PRESS/NEW YORK TIMES COLLECTION

SERIES I

Abbott, Edith.
Women in Industry. 1913.

Aveling, Edward B. and Eleanor M. Aveling.
Working Class Movement in America. 1891.

Beard, Mary.
The American Labor Movement. 1939.

Blankenhorn, Heber.
The Strike for Union. 1924.

Blum, Solomon.
Labor Economics. 1925.

Brandeis, Louis D. and Josephine Goldmark.
Women in Industry. 1907. New introduction by Leon Stein and Philip Taft.

Brooks, John Graham.
American Syndicalism. 1913.

Butler, Elizabeth Beardsley.
Women and the Trades. 1909.

Byington, Margaret Frances.
Homestead: The Household of A Mill Town. 1910.

Carroll, Mollie Ray.
Labor and Politics. 1923.

Coleman, McAlister.
Men and Coal. 1943.

Coleman, J. Walter.
The Molly Maguire Riots: Industrial Conflict in the Pennsylvania Coal Region. 1936.

Commons, John R.
Industrial Goodwill. 1919.

Commons, John R.
Industrial Government. 1921.

Dacus, Joseph A.
Annals of the Great Strikes. 1877.

Dealtry, William.
The Laborer: A Remedy for his Wrongs. 1869.

Douglas, Paul H., Curtis N. Hitchcock and Willard E. Atkins, editors.
The Worker in Modern Economic Society. 1923.

Eastman, Crystal.
Work Accidents and the Law. 1910.

Ely, Richard T.
The Labor Movement in America. 1890. New Introduction by Leon Stein and Philip Taft.

Feldman, Herman.
Problems in Labor Relations. 1937.

Fitch, John Andrew.
The Steel Worker. 1910.

Furniss, Edgar S. and Laurence Guild.
Labor Problems. 1925.

Gladden, Washington.
Working People and Their Employers. 1885.

Gompers, Samuel.
Labor and the Common Welfare. 1919.

Hardman, J. B. S., editor.
American Labor Dynamics. 1928.

Higgins, George G.
Voluntarism in Organized Labor, 1930-40. 1944.

Hiller, Ernest T.
The Strike. 1928.

Hollander, Jacob S. and George E. Barnett.
Studies in American Trade Unionism. 1906. New Introduction by Leon Stein and Philip Taft.

Jelley, Symmes M.
The Voice of Labor. 1888.

Jones, Mary.
Autobiography of Mother Jones. 1925.

Kelley, Florence.
Some Ethical Gains Through Legislation. 1905.

LaFollette, Robert M., editor.
The Making of America: Labor. 1906.

Lane, Winthrop D.
Civil War in West Virginia. 1921.

Lauck, W. Jett and Edgar Sydenstricker.
Conditions of Labor in American Industries. 1917.

Leiserson, William M.
Adjusting Immigrant and Industry. 1924.

Lescohier, Don D.
Knights of St. Crispin. 1910.

Levinson, Edward.
I Break Strikes. The Technique of Pearl L. Bergoff. 1935.

Lloyd, Henry Demarest.
Men, The Workers. Compiled by Anne Whithington and Caroline Stallbohen. 1909. New Introduction by Leon Stein and Philip Taft.

Lorwin, Louis (Louis Levine).
The Women's Garment Workers. 1924.

Markham, Edwin, Ben B. Lindsay and George Creel.
Children in Bondage. 1914.

Marot, Helen.
American Labor Unions. 1914.

Mason, Alpheus T.
Organized Labor and the Law. 1925.

Newcomb, Simon.
A Plain Man's Talk on the Labor Question. 1886. New Introduction by Leon Stein and Philip Taft.

Price, George Moses.
The Modern Factory: Safety, Sanitation and Welfare. 1914.

Randall, John Herman Jr.
Problem of Group Responsibility to Society. 1922.

Rubinow, I. M.
Social Insurance. 1913.

Saposs, David, editor.
Readings in Trade Unionism. 1926.

Slichter, Sumner H.
Union Policies and Industrial Management. 1941.

Socialist Publishing Society.
The Accused and the Accusers. 1887.

Stein, Leon and Philip Taft, editors.
The Pullman Strike. 1894-1913. New Introduction by the editors.

Stein, Leon and Philip Taft, editors.
Religion, Reform, and Revolution: Labor Panaceas in the Nineteenth Century. 1969. New Introduction by the editors.

Stein, Leon and Philip Taft, editors.
Wages, Hours, and Strikes: Labor Panaceas in the Twentieth Century. 1969. New introduction by the editors.

Swinton, John.
A Momentous Question: The Respective Attitudes of Labor and Capital. 1895. New Introduction by Leon Stein and Philip Taft.

Tannenbaum, Frank.
The Labor Movement. 1921.

Tead, Ordway.
Instincts in Industry. 1918.

Vorse, Mary Heaton.
Labor's New Millions. 1938.

Witte, Edwin Emil.
The Government in Labor Disputes. 1932.

Wright, Carroll D.
The Working Girls of Boston. 1889.

Wyckoff, Veitrees J.
Wage Policies of Labor Organizations in a Period of Industrial Depression. 1926.

Yellen, Samuel.
American Labor Struggles. 1936.

SERIES II

Allen, Henry J.
The Party of the Third Part: The Story of the Kansas Industrial Relations Court. 1921. *Including* **The Kansas Court of Industrial Relations Law** (1920) by Samuel Gompers.

Baker, Ray Stannard.
The New Industrial Unrest. 1920.

Barnett, George E. & David A. McCabe.
Mediation, Investigation and Arbitration in Industrial Disputes. 1916.

Barns, William E., editor.
The Labor Problem. 1886.

Bing, Alexander M.
War-Time Strikes and Their Adjustment. 1921.

Brooks, Robert R. R.
When Labor Organizes. 1937.

Calkins, Clinch.
Spy Overhead: The Story of Industrial Espionage. 1937.

Cooke, Morris Llewellyn & Philip Murray.
Organized Labor and Production. 1940.

Creamer, Daniel & Charles W. Coulter.
Labor and the Shut-Down of the Amoskeag Textile Mills. 1939.

Glocker, Theodore W.
The Government of American Trade Unions. 1913.

Gompers, Samuel.
Labor and the Employer. 1920.

Grant, Luke.
The National Erectors' Association and the International Association of Bridge and Structural Ironworkers. 1915.

Haber, William.
Industrial Relations in the Building Industry. 1930.

Henry, Alice.
Women and the Labor Movement. 1923.

Herbst, Alma.
The Negro in the Slaughtering and Meat-Packing Industry in Chicago. 1932.

[Hicks, Obediah.]
Life of Richard F. Trevellick. 1896.

Hillquit, Morris, Samuel Gompers & Max J. Hayes.
The Double Edge of Labor's Sword: Discussion and Testimony on Socialism and Trade-Unionism Before the Commission on Industrial Relations. 1914. New Introduction by Leon Stein and Philip Taft.

Jensen, Vernon H.
Lumber and Labor. 1945.

Kampelman, Max M.
The Communist Party vs. the C.I.O. 1957.

Kingsbury, Susan M., editor.
Labor Laws and Their Enforcement. By Charles E. Persons, Mabel Parton, Mabelle Moses & Three "Fellows." 1911.

McCabe, David A.
The Standard Rate in American Trade Unions. 1912.

Mangold, George Benjamin.
Labor Argument in the American Protective Tariff Discussion. 1908.

Millis, Harry A., editor.
How Collective Bargaining Works. 1942.

Montgomery, Royal E.
Industrial Relations in the Chicago Building Trades. 1927.

Oneal, James.
The Workers in American History. 3rd edition, 1912.

Palmer, Gladys L.
Union Tactics and Economic Change: A Case Study of Three Philadelphia Textile Unions. 1932.

Penny, Virginia.
How Women Can Make Money: Married or Single, In all Branches of the Arts and Sciences, Professions, Trades, Agricultural and Mechanical Pursuits. 1870. New Introduction by Leon Stein and Philip Taft.

Penny, Virginia.
Think and Act: A Series of Articles Pertaining to Men and Women, Work and Wages. 1869.

Pickering, John.
The Working Man's Political Economy. 1847.

Ryan, John A.
A Living Wage. 1906.

Savage, Marion Dutton.
Industrial Unionism in America. 1922.

Simkhovitch, Mary Kingsbury.
The City Worker's World in America. 1917.

Spero, Sterling Denhard.
The Labor Movement in a Government Industry: A Study of Employee Organization in the Postal Service. 1927.

Stein, Leon and Philip Taft, editors.
Labor Politics: Collected Pamphlets. 2 vols. 1836-1932. New Introduction by the editors.

Stein, Leon and Philip Taft, editors.
The Management of Workers: Selected Arguments. 1917-1956. New Introduction by the editors.

Stein, Leon and Philip Taft, editors.
Massacre at Ludlow: Four Reports. 1914-1915. New Introduction by the editors.

Stein, Leon and Philip Taft, editors.
Workers Speak: Self-Portraits. 1902-1906. New Introduction by the editors.

Stolberg, Benjamin.
The Story of the CIO. 1938.

Taylor, Paul S.
The Sailors' Union of the Pacific. 1923.

U.S. Commission on Industrial Relations.
Efficiency Systems and Labor. 1916. New Introduction by Leon Stein and Philip Taft.

Walker, Charles Rumford.
American City: A Rank-and-File History. 1937.

Walling, William English.
American Labor and American Democracy. 1926.

Williams, Whiting.
What's on the Worker's Mind: By One Who Put on Overalls to Find Out. 1920.

Wolman, Leo.
The Boycott in American Trade Unions. 1916.

Ziskind, David.
One Thousand Strikes of Government Employees. 1940.